Living
Toad Free

Also available from Leadership Development Press by
Dan Bobinski and Dennis Rader:

*The Teacher's Intellect; Creating Conditions
for Teaching and Learning*

Living Toad Free

*Overcoming Resistance
to Motivation*

Dan Bobinski
Dennis Rader

LEADERSHIP
DEVELOPMENT
PRESS

A Division of LEADERSHIP DEVELOPMENT, Inc.

Living Toad Free
Dan Bobinski and Dennis Rader

Published by Leadership Development Press
a division of Leadership Development, Inc.
P.O. Box 4082, Boise, ID 83711

Toll Free 888-922-6224

Printed in the United States of America

ISBN 1-594674-80-9

Printed by Xulon Press, Inc.

Artwork by Doug England.

Bible quotations are taken from the HOLY BIBLE, NEW INTERNATIONAL VERSION, Copyright © 1973, 1978, 1984 International Bible Society. Used by permission of Zondervan Bible Publishers.

Content in all stories has been altered to protect the innocent – and the guilty.

iv

ATTENTION SCHOOLS AND CORPORATIONS:

Books from Leadership Development Press are available at quantity discounts with bulk purchase for educational, business, fundraising, or promotional use. For information, please contact Leadership Development Press at the address or telephone number listed on the preceding page.

For Todd
of the *Dead Poets Society*
And in memory of Neil,
who could not get past his Toads

Acknowledgements

As much as we'd like to acknowledge everyone who contributed to this work, it would be impossible. Friends, teachers, pastors, family members, and even actors playing roles in movies have helped both of us in our quests to live Toad Free.

But there are a few people that we absolutely must thank: Lorena Bobinski, Noriko Tsuchiya, Judy Paxton, Alex Goodman, Travis Whitman, Anita Miller, Lesa Horrocks, Robert Croker, Greg Sigerson, Ana Hollinger, and Bill Levy.

Additionally, we would like to thank all of our students and clients who have shared with us their Toad stories over the years.

And as we say around the office, "whoever dies with the most dead Toads, wins."

x

Living Toad Free

TABLE OF CONTENTS

INTRODUCTION

As we put the finishing touches on this book, we are spending a few days away from our daily routines at a hotel in Northern Kentucky. It's early spring, and outside the window of our hotel is a large green meadow framed against the backdrop of newly reborn green trees and beautiful rolling hills. Every morning the robins descend on the meadow and spend the day looking for worms and eating bugs.

In reflecting on these birds, we were reminded that God provides for all creatures. In the case of the robins, worms and bugs are provided daily, but the worms are not dropped in the robin's nests. These birds have to get out there and look for their food.

By the same token, these birds are looking for food in a real meadow, not on Astroturf. They might have looked around on Astroturf at one point in time but soon learned it is futile to keep looking for nourishment in places where it does not exist!

By definition, the word "motivation" means "a reason to move." If worms were piped straight to the robin's nests, their bellies would be full but their hearts and wings would atrophy. Robins know they have to move to get their food. They also know where they have to go to get it. Their reasons for movement are clear and consistent.

Humans, on the other hand, move for reasons that are less clear and consistent. Sometimes we find ourselves looking for spiritual nourishment in what for us is the equivalent of Astroturf. When that happens, we run the danger of becoming misdirected, and striving to become what we were never meant to be.

Parker Palmer, in his book *Let Your Life Speak: Listening for the Voice of Vocation*, was certain that he had been called to become a minister:

> So it came as a great shock, at the end of my first year [in seminary], God spoke to me—in the form of mediocre grades and massive misery—and informed me that under no conditions was I to become an ordained leader in His church.

Palmer went off to eventually find his true calling, as a teacher and a writer. Whenever resistance fights against the force of your motivation, you have to find out why. Is it something destructive inside yourself, or is it God's way of saying that the endeavor is not your vocation? Palmer writes:

Vocation does not come from willingness. It comes from listening. I must listen to my life and try to understand what it is truly about – quite apart from what I would like it to be about – or my life will never represent anything real in the world, no matter how earnest my intentions.

That insight is hidden in the word vocation, which is rooted in the Latin for "voice." Vocation does not mean a goal that I pursue. It means a calling that I hear. Before I can tell my life what I want to do with it, I must listen to my life telling me who I am.

We can safely assume that when we identify the kind of "food" designed for us, we won't find ourselves stymied by Toady conditions. In other words, the flow of our life gets easier when we align ourselves with our vocation.

Our concern in *Living Toad Free* is with those situations in which we encounter resistance to motivation. While motivation is a reason to move, resistance is what impedes flow. We call these impediments Toads because it helps us visualize them. (They are then easier to identify and squash.) Toads prevent us from becoming who we should become; they are self-defeating beliefs and behaviors that we receive from others or generate and nourish ourselves.

Robins have no inner resistance to looking for food (their fulfillment). If physically healthy, they are out there every day hard at work. But when internal resistance impedes our flow in the pursuit of our motivations, we need to ask "why?"

Are we striving to do the wrong thing, something not connected to our vocation? Or are we harboring and nourishing Toads, unconsciously resisting our innate desire to move toward our potential?

It is our hope that this book will help us find fulfillment in our vocations as well as eliminate the Toads that prevent us from answering the call to those vocations. There is much wisdom in learning to listen for the voice of your true calling, as well as learning how to ignore the ugly voices of Toads.

By the way, in another unique parallel, we find it ironic that just as Palmer says we must listen for our calling, robins do not scratch and peck for worms and bugs; they "listen" and look carefully to find the nourishment they need. Bottom line, fulfillment begins with listening.

> Dan Bobinski and Dennis Rader
> Northern Kentucky
> March, 2004

Overview:

The first part of this book is about helping you recognize Toads for what they are. We've also included a section with tips for how to eliminate Toads from your life. In Appendix B you'll find a suggested reading list to help expand your Toad-eliminating skills.

I set before you life or death, blessing or curse.
Therefore, choose life.
- Deuteronomy 30:19

SECTION ONE

THE TOAD CONCEPT

Chapter 1

THE COACH HATFIELD STORY

You can outdistance that which is running after you,
but not what is running inside you.
- Rwandan Proverb

Coach Hatfield knew about Toads. He knew where they came from, but more importantly he knew how to get rid of them. The key, according to Coach Hatfield, was to figure out what Toads were getting in the way, then eliminate them.

Coach Hatfield was a basketball coach at a small college in Illinois. He was tough, but he let everybody play. Most folks said he worked miracles, because somehow he developed winning teams in a school too small to really have the horses. But the "miracles" that occurred were simply a result of the way he taught his teams to view life.

At the beginning of every season Coach Hatfield sat down with the new players and told them the following story:

Mr. Centipede woke up early one morning in a great mood. He had a date later that day with the centipede of his dreams, Ms. Diana Centipede! She had one hundred of the longest legs he'd ever seen.

Mr. Centipede showered, put on his favorite yellow socks and fifty pairs of black Adidas tennis shoes. He slicked back his hair, flashed himself a confident smile in the mirror and headed for the door. With every leg in perfect rhythm, he flowed out of his little cave on the side of the hill.

As fate would have it, Mr. Centipede chanced upon Mr. Toad, sitting by the side of the trail (on a toadstool, of course), in his usual toady frame of mind. Mr. Centipede, beaming confidence, stopped and raised ten of his legs in a friendly salute. 'Good Morning, Mr. Toad! How are you on this gorgeous day?'

Mr. Toad gave Mr. Centipede an aggravated glance, then grumbled back. 'What's so good about it?'

Realizing he didn't want to lose his good mood in debating with a Toad, Mr. Centipede turned his head and answered to the air about the bright sun, the puffy clouds, and the fresh air. Then, starting up his jaunty, rippling body once again, and with all his legs in perfect rhythm, he flowed past Mr. Toad.

That's when it happened. Mr. Toad's brow furled as he watched Mr. Centipede glide past. Then a quizzical look came over the toad's scowling face as he called out to Mr. Centipede in a gruff, toady voice. 'Mr. Centipede! Stop! There's something I want to ask you.'

Mr. Centipede stopped mid-stride, looked back over his shoulder, and said, 'What is it, Mr. Toad?'

'How do you do it, Mr. Centipede?'

'Do what?'

'Walk! How do you walk with all those legs in perfect unison? How in the world do you manage to move them all, much less at the same time?'

Mr. Centipede tilted his head and thought about the question. And he thought. And then he thought some more. Mr. Centipede missed his date. In fact, Mr. Centipede never moved again!

Then Coach Hatfield explained to his newcomers how Sammy Centipede had encountered a Toad of Confusion. "The Toad," Coach explained, "sent the centipede's state of mind into a whirlwind of doubt and confusion, totally taking him off guard. So much so that he froze—which made him lose his potential for fulfillment."

The new ballplayers nodded as if they understood, but Coach Hatfield wasn't done yet. He showed them a plaque with a saying engraved on it:

> It's no sin to be blocked.
> Only to stay blocked.

Then Coach Hatfield would say, "There are a lot of Toads and Toady situations in life that trip us up. Fear Toads, Perfection Toads, Inferiority Toads, Superiority Toads, Intimidation Toads, Guilt Toads, you name 'em, they're out there! We've all got our share of Toads, but that's okay. What's not okay is to let any Toad, small or large, grow so big that it cripples us. The worst Toads, the biggest ones, are those that we feed and care for ourselves—the ones we grow with our own thoughts."

The players were looking a bit confused, so Coach Hatfield threw the facts straight at them: "There are two kinds of basketball players. One is the guy fooling around on the playground. He isn't serious. Either he isn't committed or he hasn't got the guts or the brains to nurture his talent. The other kind has the courage and the fortitude to challenge the Toads preventing him from being the best he can be. Those without the dedication, the courage, or the perseverance to eliminate their Toads should go home now. You will become mature players in this game or you will be gone!

"Whenever a Toad knocks us down we're going to either get back up to knock it down or we're going to find a way around it! People who succeed at this game are just like people who succeed at life. They don't feed or pamper their Toads. Instead they find them and exterminate them! We will not allow any Toads to get in our way! Is that understood?

It was understood. The Toad concept worked to bring the teams together every year. In fact, the shout of "Kill the Toad! Kill the Toad!" became the team's rally cry, much to the confusion of opposing teams.

Coach Hatfield used the Toad analogy all the time. He frequently chose his starters by looking each player in the eye and asking, "Are you Toad Free tonight?" And once, when the team's best player developed an attitude of superiority, Coach Hatfield helped him become the team's best "team-player" by showing him how his ego had become a Toad to the rest of the team.

Coach Hatfield's Toad stories taught his teams about resiliency and stamina. They learned to take the heavy blows and keep on moving. Hence, they were never routed. Not only did they never quit as individuals, they "jelled" so well as a team they ended up winning games that, on paper, they weren't supposed to win. And whenever they were defeated, they were beaten by a genuinely superior team—never by themselves.

No matter what, his teams always kept their pride because they always maintained flow and momentum, keeping their integrity even in the face of overwhelming competition. Coach Hatfield called that character. No matter what the score or the reputation of the opposition, all of

Coach Hatfield's players held onto their integrity. They learned how to search for the Toads impeding their potential. And they began eliminating those Toads as soon as they found them.

Chapter 2

WHY TOADS?

Uncultivated minds are not full of wild flowers,
like uncultivated fields.
Villainous weeds grow in them
and they are the haunt of toads.
                              - Logan Pearsall Smith

What does an analogy about Toads have to do with you and your personal or professional growth? We equate "having a Toad" with having an obstacle to personal or professional development. Here are just a few comparisons of obstacles and actual toads:

Toads: Toads haven't changed much over the ages. According to the fossil record, they look pretty much the same today as they did when time began.

Obstacles: All of us have obstacles in life. They're the same kinds of problems people have been having since the dawn of time. And, just like toads, the problems holding us back can be pretty ugly.

Toads: Toads can live almost anywhere. After toad eggs hatch, they start out as seemingly insignificant tadpoles. But after the metamorphosis is complete, the tadpoles transform into full-size toads.

Obstacles: Problems and obstacles exist everywhere. And no matter where we live, events happen during our earliest years that bewilder us. (Some may even seem insignificant at the time.) From our interpretation of these events we draw conclusions—about ourselves, about others, about our situations, and about life. These conclusions are not always accurate, and down the road these incorrect conclusions can grow and prevent us from becoming all we are capable of being.

Toads: You may know of only a few types of toads, but there are dozens and dozens of toad varieties in the world in many different sizes, each with its own peculiar way of surviving.

Obstacles: The obstacles we face come in a wide variety of shapes and sizes. You may have awareness of a select group of personal issues that inhibit development. But

28

think about how many diseases (both physical and mental) and self-defeating behaviors of which you are unaware or know very little. The obstacles people face are many, each with its own way of persisting.

Some folks refer to Toads as "hang ups," "having issues," "personal problems," or "baggage." Whatever it's called, the result is a resistance to change. Psychologists often refer to these Toads as neurotic or self-defeating behavior. We call it simply *having a Toad*.

Why Toads? Well, the biggest difficulty with any resistance to growth, especially internal resistance, is that we rarely realize it exists. Others try pointing out our resistance—or problem—to us, yet we still have a tough time "seeing" it. Sometimes we're told that we have "old tapes," or "ghosts" that haunt us. Still, these concepts are vague and ambiguous.

It's hard to "see" resistance—the internal impediments to our own development. If we're lucky, we understand the problems only as vague and ambiguous ideas and grapple to get hold of the concepts. Since most people are visual learners, we don't think nebulous terms make for user-friendly methodology, especially for the person who's trying to overcome his or her problems and get on with a fulfilling life!

On the other hand, we can easily visualize a Toad. We think—and ditch this book if we're wrong—Toads are very easy to visualize in your mind. If you doubt this, try our little test:

A psychologist says that a client is suffering from agoraphobia.

Using our approach, we say the client has a big Toad sitting on his front step that won't let him go outside.

Assuming that you're not a seasoned (and jaded) psychologist, which is easier to picture mentally:
   a)   agoraphobia, or
   b)   the Toad?

If your answer is the Toad, this book is for you. (If your answer is agoraphobia, you'd better see a psychologist!)

Learning how to eliminate Toads, that is, overcoming resistance to becoming who you are meant to be, begins with identifying the type of Toad in your way. The Toad may be huge, blocking the path that takes you to your goal, or small, jumping out to trip you up or distract you every time you walk down a particular path. By eliminating the Toads' influences, usually accomplished by starving them into weakness or into disappearance, or by going around them, you can continue on your way to your calling and your goals.

What could be more visual? What could be more helpful than having an easy-to-use metaphor? All in all, it's about helping you overcome the resistance that stops you from reaching your full potential.

As best-selling author Ken Blanchard says, "I believe that deep down in all of us is a little voice that cries out 'Inspire me! Help me be the kind of person I want to be.'"

You can do it! You can eliminate the Toads in your life, and the concept in this book will help you do it. We believe everyone has the right to be *Living Toad Free*

Chapter 3

THE ORIGINAL POEM*

The centipede was happy quite,
Until a toad in fun
Said, "Pray, which leg goes after which?"
This worked his mind to such a pitch,
He lay distracted in a ditch
Considering how to run.

The actual origin of this poem is unknown, but we do know it is the poem from which Coach Hatfield created his Toad story.

~~~~~~~~~~~~~~~~~~~~~~~~~~~~~~~~~~~~~~

SECTION TWO

TOADS AT HOME

~~~~~~~~~~~~~~~~~~~~~~~~~~~~~~~~~~~~~~

Chapter 4

MIKE AND MARGARET

*It seems to me probable that anyone who has
had a series of intolerable positions to put up with
must have been responsible for them to some extent.*
- Robert Hugh Benson

Mike and Margaret were your typical, middle-class parents. Margaret, a little more ambitious and outgoing than her husband, acquired a real estate license and liked to go out and meet people by selling homes in their small suburban town. Mike, slightly built and more timid, worked as a certified mechanic at a local repair shop. He was quiet and found contentment working by himself and doing the job right.

They had two young children, Samantha and Paul. Their family was as middle-of-the road as middle class gets. Margaret made sure that the children were involved in school, while Mike made it a habit to be glued to the TV on the weekends, sip a beer or two, and quietly watch whatever sport was in season. Margaret's mother, long divorced from a deadbeat dad, lived just a few blocks away, so she visited often.

One cloudy, cool morning, Mike was working at the auto repair shop as usual. He had his head under the hood of a car when he heard someone pull up just outside the service bay. Hearing the car door slam abruptly, Mike got out from under the hood to see a very angry person walking toward him. Non-confrontational by nature, Mike politely asked the man to step outside the service bay for insurance reasons. The man gave no hint of leaving. "What's up with this place?" the man yelled. "My wife comes here with a small knock in her engine and you guys milk her for $800?"

Mike looked out past the man at his car. It had been in the shop yesterday. "I recognize the car, sir, but I wasn't the one who worked on it. Let me see if I can—"

Mike didn't have a chance to finish his sentence. The man was a ticking time bomb. "I don't care WHO worked on it, I want my money back!"

Realizing he wasn't going to get anywhere with this irate customer, Mike shook his head and turned to go get his supervisor. The irate customer, thinking he was being ignored, let his fuse run out. He picked up a large pipe wrench and threw it at the back of Mike's head. Mike awoke to a couple of paramedics kneeling over him telling him that he was going to be all right.

As it turned out, the irate customer was arrested and Mike spent a day in the hospital for observation. After Mike was released, his boss gave him a few days off, but that didn't seem to be enough. The idea of getting his head bashed in for trying to provide good customer service didn't sit well. "What's it all for?" Mike thought.

A few days turned into a few weeks. Mike told his boss that he wasn't feeling up to coming back to work. The doctors had pronounced him fit, but Mike was uncomfortable about leaving the house. In fact, Mike was so withdrawn, he wouldn't even attend his attacker's trial.

After two months, his boss stopped by to talk. "I understand you might have some hesitancy about dealing with customers, but I need you at the shop, Mike, or we're going to have to let you go so I can hire somebody else."

Mike just stared at the wall. Silence permeated the room for what seemed like an hour. Finally Mike said, "That'd be okay."

Mike's boss paused. "I'm sorry to hear that," he said. After waiting a few more moments and looking at Mike with great concern in his eyes, he continued, "If you ever need to talk, just let me know." With that, Mike's boss got up and left, and Mike sat staring at the wall.

Margaret, a little afraid but not wanting to upset her already unstable household, went to Mike the next day and told him that it didn't matter if he didn't work—she'd carry the financial load. In fact, she'd already crunched the numbers and, although it would be a squeeze, they could keep getting by on her income alone. Mike just nodded, and then said, "I'll keep up with the housework."

"Yes! That'll work!" Margaret said enthusiastically. It was an honorable way to explain the situation to their neighbors and relatives. "You can take care of the kids and the house, and I'll go do the 9-to-5 thing! After all, we're adaptable! We can do this!"

Margaret picked up the pace at work and showed more homes to compensate for the loss of Mike's income. Longer hours were okay in her mind, as long as she didn't let her family fall apart, as she perceived her mother had done so many years ago. Mike mostly sat around increasing his dosage of ESPN, ESPN-2, and any other sports he could find. He took comfort in his wife saying it was okay for him to stay home. By five o'clock he had done a few chores and dinner was on the stove. Once a week, he'd venture outside to mow the lawn and do some other yard work, but his days were mostly spent reading the newspaper and watching TV.

The children, Samantha and Paul, now in the third and fourth grades, were excited that Dad was going to be around when they got home from school. Now he could do things with them in the early afternoon, where before they were pretty much on their own. Their excitement waned as they discovered that Dad wasn't going to be all that involved, but they were still glad he was around.

Inside themselves, the children were screaming for attention, but pulling Dad's eyes away from the TV was practically impossible. "I'm going to ride my bike, Daddy," Paul would often say, "Do you want to watch me?" "Sure," Mike said, without moving his eyes from the TV. Paul would run out to the garage, hop on his bike and ride it up and down the street. Each time he passed the house he would stick his hand up and wave, "Hi Daddy!" Sadly, Mike was oblivious.

After almost six months of this, Margaret stayed up late one night to talk with Mike. "Honey, I'm a little concerned," she said. "You're doing a great job of keeping up the house and all the work that needs to be done around here." She paused, and then continued, "I'm just concerned that we're a little disconnected. The kids haven't said anything, but I can see in their faces that they don't feel you care."

Mike got defensive. "Don't care? Of course I care!" he spouted. "I do their laundry, I vacuum their floors, I fix their dinner, I take care of them just fine! If that's not caring, I don't know what is!" He bristled at the thought that somehow he was inadequate.

Margaret wasn't prepared for Mike's defensive posture and loud tone of voice. Not wanting to upset the picture of a peaceful home, she backed down quickly, and quietly asked Mike to engage more with the children. "Yeah, yeah, of course," Mike replied, but both of them knew nothing was going to change.

Margaret's mother began spending extra time with the children. She tried to support Margaret as best she could. Mike, however, continued to exclude himself from the rest of the world—except for his newspaper and sports television.

Over the years, Margaret got the children involved in soccer and little league. Asking Mike to attend any of their games always resulted in a "No." The children knew better, but Margaret would always ask a second time. "Come on, Mike, when was the last time you saw the kids play?" But Mike's regular reply was "I don't feel like going," and his voice tone always indicated that his decision was final.

Once Margaret even suggested that she and Mike go in for some marital counseling. "Not on your life," Mike replied. "We're doing just fine. The bills are getting paid, the house is kept up, and nothing needs fixing—in the house or in the marriage."

The world went by, and Mike continued down his path of self-defined peaceful existence, unencumbered by the troubles of day-to-day work or family issues. The children went on to graduate high school, but Mike found a reason for not attending either ceremony.

Eventually the nest was empty and Margaret and Mike were at home alone. Margaret put away money for herself and started taking little vacations every few months, by herself. She would always stay faithful, as she didn't want her marriage—what little there was of it—to break up like her mother's had. But after the kids were gone, Margaret felt like she was one of the loneliest people on the face of the planet.

Thoughts:
As is usually the case, more than one Toad exists in this story. When Mike was assaulted, a Toad jumped on him and told him to stay away from people. That Toad then invited other Toads to join in the fun of freezing Mike's potential, of separating him from his life. Mike did nothing to stop them. Perhaps in Mike's youth he was never told he could shake off the Toads. Perhaps a Toad jumped on him and said that he needed Toads to be safe. Often times, Toads compel us to dig ourselves into holes and then convince us of their comfort.

Whatever the reason, Mike chose to keep Toads around and feed them. They got comfortable, convincing Mike that he should continue to feed them – for if they were comfortable, Mike would never again have to experience the possibilities of risk, fear, or loss. Unfortunately, Mike believed their lies. He believed his marriage was just fine. Intentional ignorance guaranteed his sense of safety.

Margaret couldn't bear the thought of letting her family fall apart. Her parent's breakup so many years before had given birth to a Toad that told her she shouldn't let anything come between her and her husband. Her determination led her to neglect healthy boundaries and responsibilities in the family, but at what expense? The opposite of development is diminishment. She could say that she didn't let her family fall apart, but, in reality, that is exactly what happened.

If we are parents, we have the responsibility to be good parents. If we are workers, we have the responsibility to be good workers. If we are spouses, we have the responsibility to be good spouses. We can be sympathetic to the plight of Margaret and Mike, but perhaps even more sympathetic for their children

Chapter 5

TWIN TOADS OF DIFFERENT MOTHERS

*Men can starve from a lack of self-realization
as much as they can from a lack of bread.*
- Richard Wright

Helen's story:

In the upper middle class circles of my Massachusetts upbringing, it was clear my parents believed
family reputation came first. My mother and father de-
voted their time to the country club and social events. It
sometimes felt like my needs took a back seat, but I believed they were doing the right thing. My mother taught
me a lot about what a woman should do.

Yet despite all the talk and appearance of family love,
long arguments and criticism were common at my house.
Father said good arguing kept us sharp, but it was to be
contained within the family. It made sense to me, so I
never mentioned it to anyone.

Mother was especially critical of everything I did. She told me that she was just making sure I would grow up to be a strong woman. I so desired to do right that I went along with it. Even if I had an argument with my parents and we then went outside and ran into a neighbor a few minutes later, everything would have to appear sugary sweet among us. After all, we were a loving, stable family, and outsiders had no need to know of our personal matters.

I attended an Ivy League college, earned a master's degree, and then got a prestigious position at a Fortune 500 company. The business social scene became the centerpiece of everything I did. I dedicated myself to my work and my involvement with several service organizations.

Unfortunately, it seemed I would never marry. I dated on and off, but somehow seemed to intimidate all the men I met. Before I knew it, I was 34 and still single.

Finally I met Craig. He had only an associate's degree and had bounced around in different career fields, which bothered me at first. But I liked him. Mother said that Craig was probably an irresponsible, playboy bachelor. "After all," she once told me, "he's 29 and doesn't have a stable career!" Even though my parents were against our marriage, I thought Craig needed someone like me in his life. Looking back, though, I wish I had known how difficult he was going to be. I never would have married him.

Craig's story:

I met Helen at a symphony concert. She showed an interest in my life, and, since I was new in town, I took a quick interest in her interest.

I'd recently landed a job as a department manager in a high-end department store and was working hard to make something of my life. Helen seemed to come from a good upbringing. "Maybe," I thought, "if I marry someone like Helen I can get away from "the wrath of Mom."

Ah, yes—Mom. Always sticking her nose in my business, wanting to know what I was up to so she could tell me what to do. I wish my dad had taught me a few things about being a man, but he always deferred to mom. And all she ever said was "Don't make waves." I still cringe at her "shoulds" and "oughts." I wish I had a dime for every time mom told me "you should" or "you ought to..." Then there's the ever popular, "because I said so," even into my adult years.

I bolted right after high school to get away from the family—took a bus to Washington D.C. where I got a job in construction. I learned a few skills and made a few friends, but construction life was not my cup of tea. I got out after one season and dinked around taking classes at a junior college in Virginia.

I wasn't sure what I wanted to do for a career, but my mom's nagging me to get a job "no matter what" put pressure on me. I didn't have a clue about what I wanted to do with my life. Her oft-repeated sentence rang through my head on a regular basis: "Get a job, get married, and everything will be okay." That was her formula—not that it worked for her and dad.

When I met Helen, I liked that she was friendly and outgoing. She was comfortable meeting people, whereas I preferred to sit in the shadows. I figured I could learn a lot from her. She had a few quirks, but I thought I could overlook her peculiarities.

Two weeks before the wedding, I got into a huge argument with Helen's mother. She wanted me to continue my education and get more involved in socially-relevant activities. She didn't seem to realize she was insulting me left and right, implying that I was incompetent.

It shocked me when Helen sided with her mother. I was furious. I couldn't believe my ears! I wanted to call off the wedding, but the invitations had already been sent out. I decided I shouldn't make waves and upset my family who had already bought airline tickets. So the wedding continued as planned. Besides, in the back of my mind I thought maybe Helen's mom was right.

Two weeks after the wedding, I realized I should have made waves. My life became a virtual hell of verbal and emotional abuse. I shouldn't have cared about the lousy few hundred bucks for people's airfare. You just can't put a price on sanity.

After three years of living hell, I couldn't take it anymore. Helen and I split and then divorced. I just couldn't take all her cutting remarks about how inept I was and how wrong I was every time I disagreed with her. If I said black, she said white. If I said white, she said black. Even after seeing numerous counselors, she wouldn't let up. I had to leave before I killed myself.

Jerry's story:

Craig was a buddy I met while working construction. He was alright, but also the kind of guy who was always telling me how I "ought" to be doing something when he wasn't so sure himself. I handled it okay. We both got out of the construction business about the same time, and then wound up taking some classes together at the local college.

When Craig told me about his relationship with Helen, I kept a "wait and see" approach. I knew Craig had been through a few women before. I had watched him screw up relationships with women who would have been wonderful partners for him. I thought he had a few things to learn

49

about giving and receiving love. Besides, Helen was from upper class society, and Craig wasn't.

My wait and see approach was wise: Helen turned me off the moment I met her. She was very controlling and treated me like I shouldn't do anything without her approval. "Wow," I thought. "This is going to be the match made in Hades." Unfortunately, every time I expressed my concern to Craig he just brushed me off.

Against my better judgment, but out of friendship with Craig, I was best man at their wedding. The ceremony and reception seemed to set the tone for their entire marriage. Craig was tense, and Helen kept telling him to lighten up. And their mothers were like birds of a feather. They both wanted to be in control. The tension created by both of their mothers was so thick you could cut it with a knife.

Their marriage lasted almost three years, but my involvement with them stopped after just six months. From the start, I couldn't stand Helen's constant opinion about what I should or shouldn't be doing. And although Craig spoke ill of his home life when the two of us got together, he kept indicating I shouldn't make waves whenever we were with his wife. It was crazy. I can't see how anything is worth playing all those games.

Thoughts:

Both Helen's and Craig's upbringing taught them to adopt their mothers' Toads. Helen's mom gave her a "Portray a Loving Family" Toad, while Craig's mom gave him a "Don't Make Waves" Toad. Plus, both mothers planted and nurtured an Approval Dependency Toad in each child. In the end, the dynamics between Helen and Craig guaranteed a sham of a marriage.

Living Toad Free does not mean hiding from negative factors. It means that if you really want something to happen, you find a way to make it so. If Helen and Craig had individually found the courage to face the Approval Dependency Toad that was sucking the life out of their marriage, then perhaps their love would have had a chance. Intentional ignorance or cowardly inaction are never good responses: Toads must be recognized for what they are in order to be dealt with effectively.

Both Craig and Helen could have benefited from the courage to listen to their friends, or engage in some honest self-confrontation, such as going to individual therapy, one-on-one coaching, or perhaps a discipleship program in their church.

.

~~~~~~~~~~~~~~~~~~~~~~~~~~~~~~~~

TOAD FUNERAL NOTICE

~~~~~~~~~~~~~~~~~~~~~~~~~~~~~~~~

In this book we include stories in which Toads are still at work and those in which Toads have passed on. For those stories in which Toads are still alive (such as in Mike and Margaret and Twin Toads of Different Mothers), we have added a postscript section entitled "Thoughts." In these thoughts we pose questions and consider alternatives available for the people portrayed in the stories.

In the Toad Funerals, those stories in which Toads have passed on (or are on the way out), we usually let the situation speak for itself. You may find an occasional postscript "Note," but, for the most part, the stories are clear about how a Toad was eliminated or avoided.

Toad Funeral #1

Chapter 6

MY TOUGHEST TOAD

*If you are distressed by anything external, the pain
is not due to the thing itself, but to your own estimate of it;
and this you have the power to revoke at any moment.*
                                                    - Marcus Aurelius

Jonathon's story:

I wasn't born with a golden spoon in my mouth, but I have had a good life. Everything has gone as planned with relatively few deviations. I grew up in a large family, poor as worldly things go but rich in experiences with family and friends. In particular, I enjoyed working with my Dad. My parents divorced when I was small but my Dad was always there even though I didn't live with him. He had his own business and I grew up working alongside him. If I needed help emotionally, spiritually, or financially, he was always there to smooth the path.

I married the perfect girl, started a family, and began a successful career. Dad went through some rough times, going through a divorce from his second wife, retirement, and eventually an illness that slowed him way down. Still, for me, things seemed fine, and I thought it was great when Dad moved next to me so that I, along with my family, could take care of him.

Eventually, Dad became even more ill. He had a mild stroke, became addicted to some of the medications that were supposed to help him, and even had periods of hallucinations. Yet still, at this point, I was optimistic that he would get better. We consulted other doctors and got him different medications. Dad was strong. He had overcome a lifetime of obstacles. Surely he could overcome this.

November 2, 1998. My brother, his family, and my wife's parents were at my house for Sunday dinner and to celebrate my 8-year old daughter's baptism. Dad was too sick to attend, so we sent a plate of food over with my 12-year old son so Dad could at least enjoy the food.

Enter the Toad.

My son soon came running back. His grandfather was on the floor with his head bleeding.

Slow motion. Blurred vision. We all ran the 75 yards to his mobile home. I got there first. Saw him...saw the blood...saw the .22 rifle that he had taught me to hunt with 30 years before.

It would be a gross understatement to say my life changed at that moment. Everything that ever made sense to me was gone. Attempting to make sense out of the situation was fruitless. I can only describe the effects of this Toad as falling into the deepest, darkest pit one can imagine. I was swimming in mud, unable to breathe. Months and months of reliving, re-enacting, re-writing the script. It never changed though. The ending always came out the same, no matter how much I tried to change it.

I've always been a Toad killer. I welcome challenge, I welcome obstacles, and I welcome mountains to climb. I tell my wife that I'm more comfortable when we are struggling with money or some other hardship because it makes me work harder. When things are too easy I get antsy.

This Toad, however, was different. It wouldn't die. I came at it from all angles. I sought God, blamed God, hated God. I sought counseling. I turned more inward than I ever had before. I closed off my own wife and children for months, even though I knew that was the worst thing to do. I didn't care.

The name of this Toad, of course, was Guilt. There was no doubt in my mind that it was my fault Dad ended his own life. I was, after all, his caregiver. I had fed him, medicated him, and even dressed him at times. I was "responsible." How could I be so careless as to allow this to happen?

This story is not over. The Guilt Toad still appears from time to time. I wrestle with him now and then, but that's an improvement because we wrestled non-stop for about a year. Now it's only every month or two, and the wrestling sessions are getting shorter and shorter. And even though it's a struggle, I always win.

I may never kill this Toad, but one thing is for sure: This is my toughest Toad. All other Toads I meet along the road pale in comparison. I can kill them in a millisecond.

As a result of facing the Guilt Toad, I've become stronger, more resolute. I stopped blaming God. I seek Him once again. I realize it is He who has brought me full circle back to normality. I've also reconnected with my family, gaining a new appreciation of their importance to me.

It has been a long road, and I don't want to travel it again. On the other hand, I realize that this Toad could have destroyed me had I let it. But now I have hope back, I have God back, and I have my family back.

Toad Funeral #2

Chapter 7

THE CHOICE FOR INTEGRITY

*When you get right down to the root of the meaning of
the word "succeed," you find it simply means to follow through.*
- F. W. Nichol

Andy's story:

Out of all the many obstacles I have overcome, it is easy to pick out the one that affected my life more than anything else. It all started on Memorial Day, 1982. My parents had dropped by to see our son, Jason, for the first time since he was born.

After they left, I sat down on the couch and my wife went to start a bath. While the tub was filling she went to the kitchen to get something to drink. All of a sudden we heard a scream coming from the bathroom: Our young son had crawled from his bedroom to the bathroom and somehow managed to get in the tub. On top of that, he had turned the water all the way to hot.

Jason was burned from his diapers down and had some burns on his arms. We took him to the hospital where, after two days, they finally admitted they did not have the expertise to help such a young child with ten percent of his body covered with third degree burns. He was life-flighted to the university medical center in the bordering state where he spent the next 60 days in the intensive care unit. Jason received many skin grafts and numerous other types of therapy.

When he finally was able to leave the Burn Center, they gave us a bill of over half a million dollars. Since our insurance covered only 80%, the situation created an immediate debt of $120,000, accompanied by the cost of several follow up surgeries, lots of prescriptions, and physical therapy.

At the same time all this was happening, my employer thought that I had been gone for too long from my job, so he thought it would be better if I just stayed gone. (This happened before passage of the Family Medical Leave Act.)

My wife and I were both from proud families that would neither accept help from anyone nor file bankruptcy, so we didn't. Instead, I found a new job and we spent the next ten years fighting bill collectors. I even had a sheriff come out to where I worked and attach my wages, which really humiliated and embarrassed me.

To make ends meet, we did most all of the physical therapy ourselves, made token payments to all the doctors and hospitals, and persevered through it. We never went out because we would have felt too guilty about all the money we owed. We didn't see it as if we had any choice. Life goes on.

This is not to say it was easy. My wife and I both blamed each other, along with ourselves. We even blamed the new hot water heater that was installed three days before the accident. I can assure you that placing blame does not cure problems nor help you get over your obstacles.

We went through a lot of hardships in those ten years, but we became a very close family because of it. We overcame our obstacles because, as I said before, we didn't see that we had any choice.

How did it all turn out? I like to keep things in perspective. My son Jason didn't talk for six weeks after he was burned, but last year he took the state championship in five different speech categories. How's that for a turnaround? This year he is the student body president at the State University. His legs are still not much to look at, but that doesn't get him down.

My wife and I both have good jobs and, except for our mortgage, we now owe no one. We also never had to declare bankruptcy and our credit is A1.

In all the obstacles that I have encountered so far, I have found that you can put them off, but they do not go away. You have to face them sooner or later. It doesn't matter if you go over, under, around, or through the obstacle, you will find that a solution exists. Who knows? You may even learn by it. It could even make you a better person.

Chapter 8

WEAN YOURSELF

Little by little, wean yourself.
This is the gist of what I have to say.

From an embryo, whose nourishment comes from blood,
Move on to an infant, drinking milk,
To a child on solid food,
To a searcher after wisdom,
To a hunter of more invisible game.

Think how it is to have a conversation with an embryo.
You might say, "the world outside is vast and intricate.
There are wheat fields and mountain passes,
And orchards in bloom.

At night there are millions of galaxies, and in sunlight
The beauty of friends dancing at a wedding."

You ask the embryo why he, or she, stays cooped up
In the dark with eyes closed.
Listen to the answer:

There is no "other world."
I know only what I've experienced.
You must be hallucinating.

- Rumi

Living Toad Free

SECTION THREE

TOADS AT SCHOOL

Chapter 9

THE SUPPRESSION OF LISA

The authority of those who teach
is often an obstacle to those who want to learn.
- Cicero

D r. Morris first met Lisa when visiting one of his student teachers at an elementary school in Florida. When he entered the first grade classroom, he noted the student teacher engaged with a small group of kids in a reading exercise. The regular teacher was giving a math lesson to another, larger group. A few children were busy at their individual desks. One of these got up and came over to him.

"Hello, my name is Lisa. You must be Dr. Morris. I understand that Miss Haynes is your student. As you can see, she is very busy, but I can help you."

"Why, thank you," Dr. Morris replied, impressed with the initiative and articulateness of this little girl.

"This is the most comfortable chair in the room. From here you can observe everyone. We all love Miss Haynes, by the way." Lisa turned to leave, but politely offered, "If there is anything else that I can do for you, just let me know."

Dr. Morris expressed his appreciation and she went back over to her desk and continued working. He observed his student teacher, who was doing fine. He had no doubts about her to begin with, and it was readily apparent that she and the children worked well together. All the children were engrossed in the lesson.

Five minutes went by, then Lisa got back up from her desk and came over to him. "Perhaps you would like to talk with some of the other students? I could arrange that for you."

This initiative so intrigued Dr. Morris that he agreed that it would be a good idea. Lisa went to several of the sitting students and spoke quietly with them. One at a time, politely and quietly, each student came over to Dr. Morris to answer any questions he might have.

At the end of the school day, Dr. Morris could not wait to ask the teacher and his student about this precocious young leader who had such poise and ability when only in the first grade.

"She was like this from the very first day," informed the teacher. "She knew how to read and get along with

68

everybody. She stayed after class to offer me her services. She said she could take over one of the reading groups if that would be helpful. I didn't have the slightest doubt that she could handle it, so I gave it a try in a limited sort of way, and it has worked out. I was afraid that the other kids would find her bossy but she somehow avoids that altogether. They like her and listen to her.

Dr. Morris always looked forward to visiting the class with Lisa. He felt that she was a natural born leader. He wondered what amazing things lie ahead for her.

Everything went well for that year, but as summer approached, Lisa's teacher became concerned. She asked Dr. Morris if he had any advice for the approaching dilemma. "Both of the second grade teachers run a tight ship. I have talked with them but they both say that Lisa is a student and should be treated like one. I think they will feel a little threatened by this amazing little girl. They will fear that she is trying to take over the class to undermine them in some way."

The teacher continued, "I tried to tell them that this is not where Lisa is coming from. She just wants to be helpful and has a natural ability to organize the other kids and get things done. But they don't want to hear it. That's not the way they see students."

Dr. Morris did not know what to advise regarding their predicament. He felt Lisa's teacher had done all she could do. Students like Lisa did not fit into standard approaches to schooling, and they were threatening to teachers who were fixated on "teachers as classroom managers."

When school started up in the fall, Dr. Morris didn't have a student teacher in Lisa's second grade class, but he took the time to visit her once and checked through the window in the door a few times. Lisa was still friendly and confident, but she looked a bit anxious.

In the third year, Dr. Morris did not have a student teacher in Lisa's school. Nonetheless, he stopped by to visit her once. She seemed subdued, so much so that he asked the assistant principal about her. The assistant principal was concerned, as Lisa had not gotten along well with either her second or third grade teachers. Nothing specific—just a general attitude of resistance and resentment.

Dr. Morris often thought about Lisa. He kept in contact with her first grade teacher, who also worried about the little girl. Both he and she hoped Lisa would have better luck with her fourth grade teacher, but it was not to be. He was not able to visit Lisa's school until half-way through the school year. When he went to the office to ask about Lisa, he was informed that Lisa was no longer at the school. She had been withdrawn by her parents and was now being home schooled.

Dr. Morris met with Miss Haynes and they decided to visit Lisa at home. They set up an appointment.

Lisa's mother was friendly and cordial. She invited them into the house and offered them coffee. They could feel the tension and sadness in the home. At one point, in response to their concerns, Lisa's mother broke into tears.

"I don't know what happened to my little girl. She started school so far ahead. She could read and do math. She was confident and always so eager to help. Now she will barely come out of her room, even to meet with people who I know she likes. The doctors keep trying to tell me that she's agoraphobic, but how could that be? What happened to my little girl?"

Thoughts:
Many Toads are generated by certain facets of our educational system. Additionally, teachers who fail to understand and empathize with students who don't "fit the mold," such as Lisa, can cause horrific Toads to be born. Lisa's style of confidence and leadership capabilities do not align with the images in the heads of many teachers regarding how teaching and learning are supposed to occur. Students are supposed to sit passively at their desks, listen attentively, and take notes or follow instructions. Teachers are to stand in front of classes and talk. For these Toads to be removed, much work lies ahead.

Post Script:
Consider the possibility of the following: It's the year 2045 and the world is in a crisis. It needs a phenomenal leader, one with the capabilities to prevent World War III. But Lisa is not available—her potential had been stifled at school.

Chapter 10

THE CASE OF THE MISSING WATCH

*Nothing is rarer than a solitary lie; for lies breed like toads;
you cannot tell one but out it comes
with a hundred young ones on its back.*
- Washington Allston

It was an ordinary day in a small town classroom in East Tennessee. Although it was early March, it was warm enough for a morning break on the playground. Mrs. Roberts wore a varied collection of bracelets and watches on her wrist as she stood watching the children. She served as the safe repository of these items as her students zoomed about the playground. She had been doing this for years and never gave it a second thought, but that was all about to change.

At the end of recess, the children lined up to retrieve their bracelets and watches. Little Billy was in the line, and asked in a confused voice, "Mrs. Roberts, where is my watch?" She looked down to see that her wrists were empty except for her own watch. Then she remembered that Billy had not given her his watch, and she told him so. Billy looked confused, said, "Oh," and turned away.

At that point, Renee, another student in the class, stepped forward and announced, "Billy did give you his watch, Mrs. Roberts; I saw him do it." With this announcement, Billy also became certain that he had given Mrs. Roberts his watch. Puzzled, Mrs. Roberts directed her students back to the classroom, then took Billy down to the office to report his missing watch.

When she got back, something was wrong with the class. They were distracted. Mrs. Roberts knew why, but she didn't know what to do about it. During lunch, she overheard one of her students telling another, "Mrs. Roberts took Billy's watch." By the time lunch was over, the predicament had grown into a full-blown Toad. No more learning was going to happen that day, and if the situation wasn't resolved, it was going to become permanent.

Mrs. Roberts was curious about Renee. The little girl was normally shy, and it was out of character for her to be outspoken. Yet, she had stepped forward and intentionally lied about Billy handing over his watch. Why?

She took Renee and Billy aside and asked them both once again if they were certain. Renee repeated her assertion without hesitation, and Billy followed suit. He was now certain as well.

Mrs. Roberts needed a solution, and she needed it immediately. She took her class back out to the playground and had them sit in a circle. She then chose a couple of students that she trusted absolutely and spread them out to search the playground for the watch. She took Billy by the hand and instructed him to retrace his steps. He told her that he had jumped immediately into a ball game. "And what were you doing before that?" she asked, "I was carrying a book from the library," Billy replied. "And where did you put the book while you were playing?" she asked. "Over here by this bush," Billy said, as he walked in that direction.

There, by the bush, was the watch.

Billy immediately apologized to Mrs. Roberts and then told the class about his mistake. But Renee did not apologize. Even when confronted with proof of her lie, she glared back at Mrs. Roberts with a frozen, stubborn stare. The predicament was not over.

Mrs. Roberts did not know what to do about Renee.

Thoughts:
What kind of Toad had taken up residence with this little girl Renee, and what other Toads might it spawn? Mrs. Roberts was right to call a search for the watch to halt further Toad growth. Many assume that Toads will disappear on their own if they are ignored, but that approach often allows Toads to find their comfort zone and begin claiming territory.

Usually, in younger children, the appearance of a Toad is caused by something happening in the home. Mrs. Roberts would do well to contact Renee's home and tactfully express concern for Renee's academic well being. These situations always call for the highest level of professionalism in a teacher.

Teachers face these kinds of Toads everyday. A good teacher, by the way, is a professional Toad killer.

Toad Funeral #3

Chapter 11

RUNNING THROUGH THE TOADS

It's all right to have butterflies in your stomach.
Just get them to fly in formation.
- Dr. Rob Gilbert

Ann's story:

Three or four times a week, I put on my Toad-killing armor. I change into shorts, sports bra, tank top, and running shoes. Until recently, I had no idea that this was amphibian-eliminating attire. Now when I run, instead of thump-thump-thump, I hear squish-squish-squish. The track is littered with Toad carcasses, so many that they are hard to avoid. There are the usual Toads: Malaise, Homework, and Just-don't-feel-like-it. They are easier to ignore every day, because the more I go on these Toad-killing sprees, the more miracles happen, the more evidence is amassed proving that I am not wasting my time in college.

The next set of usual Toads hop up once I start running: Side-ache, Muscle-ache, Breathlessness, and Nausea. Nausea is particularly fond of me lately. Oh, and the little one that almost looks innocent: That little Toad that says, "It's OK to quit, you've had a rough day."

Some days these guys are easier to beat than others. Some days they win, but those days are rare and I am winning the war as long as I come back for another battle.

After I've been running a few laps, other Toads appear. Usually it's things I've felt bad about the last couple days. Often it's Self-Doubt, or that not-so-little voice that says, "You're not good enough, not smart enough, or not well liked." These are the Toads wandering around in my mind, often occupying my thoughts between counting laps. But as each leg moves me down the track, I almost invariably kill, mutilate, and disintegrate the remains of the Toads that have, until recently, held me back.

Physiologically, I can explain why I enjoy running: Exercise is proven to increase endorphins, which elevate mood and combat depression. But there has to be more. Perhaps it's just spending the time untangling the knots in my mind.

I took the medical college admission test (MCAT) recently. The evening before the test I went running—against my "better" judgment. The Toads were saying, "You need this time to study!" "You're not ready!" "You have so much to stress about and be anxious over!" "This test could determine the rest of your life!" "What the hell are you doing taking a mindless run at a time like this?"

During my run, my attitude went through a metamorphosis. On the first lap I was agreeing with the Toads: I wasn't ready for the test...there was so much more to review...I wasn't smart enough to retain it...I didn't remember enough from my classes. I was sure I would bomb.

On the next lap I began to think about retaking the test if this one didn't go so well.

A few more laps and I began to focus on how well I had done on some practice tests, and—more importantly—how much I had improved with each practice test.

I felt some of the knots in my back begin to unwind, but the Toads were still there, telling me that this test was real, and would therefore be worse than the practice ones.

As I continued to run, I looked closely at strategies that had worked for me in the past, and the conditions under which I had taken the practice tests. I focused on relaxing. I told myself to focus on the material instead of what being right or wrong was going to lead to; it had nothing to do with the test itself and was only going to waste brain-power on extraneous stuff. I worked out more "winning" strategies and began to convince myself that I would do well enough. By the end of the run, I was sure I would kick butt the next day, whatever they threw at me. I was ready!

When I finally got my scores from the MCAT, they were much higher than I expected. (This is one of the miracles that keeps me going back to the gym!) Thank goodness I went for that run! In retrospect, I know I wouldn't have done nearly as well if I had taken all those Toads into the testing room with me.

Sometimes, I think I can even see Toads in other peoples' pockets, backpacks, and on their shoulders, whispering in their ears. Toads are everywhere.

I still have plenty of my own Toads. New ones find me every day as I seek out new challenges, but killing Toads is now a regular part of my life, and the more I kill, the more I want to kill. Yesterday, I killed the "I-can't-seem-to-get-past-two miles" Toad. I ran three miles in spite of a croaking chorus.

Toad Funeral #4

Chapter 12

SANTA'S DOLL

*The moment we begin to fear the opinions of others
and hesitate to tell the truth that is in us,
and from motives of policy are silent when we should speak,
the divine floods of light and life no longer flow into our souls.*
- Elizabeth Cady Stanton

Rosie's story:

I grew up in East Texas in an area they call The Big Thicket. We were poor, but I didn't think about it much until I started school. All my clothes were hand-me-downs from my older sister. They were already stained, torn, and threadbare, and everybody knew my situation. Kids notice that kind of thing, and they were not kind.

Then, when I was ten, my father was killed in a car accident (hit by a drunk driver) on his way home from work in the fields. There was, of course, no insurance, and the drunk had no money; he only spent a few months in jail and then disappeared. At the time of my father's death, my mother was five months pregnant with my sixth sibling. That made seven kids without a father. Somehow, Mom managed to support all of us and to this day I don't know how she did it.

I remember when I was in the fifth grade we were getting ready for the school Christmas program. It was a big deal and everyone was excited. The teachers from both classes in our little school wrote on the chalkboard what roles would be available and told us to think about which ones we wanted to be.

I knew instantly that I wanted to be one of the dolls. I told my best friend and she agreed that I would make a pretty doll.

That afternoon, during recess, I was playing outside when three snobby girls from my class came up to me. These girls were really popular, especially with the boys. They wore the nicest clothes and were so mean and rude to those of us who did not. The only time they spoke to me was to tease and make fun of me. They told me that I could not be one of the dolls because they only needed three and they were going to be them. And they always got their way.

"Besides," one of them said, "Santa does not make brown dolls and you never wear pretty dresses anyway."

Then one of the other girls said, "Why don't you be one of the reindeer? They are brown like you."

I felt so bad that I wanted to cry, but I didn't. I was not about to give them the satisfaction of hurting my feelings once again.

I went home that night feeling sorry for myself and started crying. The more I thought about it the more I decided they were right. I was a poor Mexican girl with no pretty dress to wear and I had no right to have a major role in our Christmas program. A program my mother wouldn't even be able to attend because she worked the night shift at the factory where they made frozen dinners.

The next day at school, our teacher asked us what we wanted to be. I had decided the night before that I was going to be either an elf or a reindeer. When she got to me, I just about said "elf" but instead I blurted out, "DOLL!"

All heads turned and looked at me because word on the playground was the doll roles were already spoken for, but in that split second my mind was made up. I was going to be a doll no matter what.

I thought, "I may be brown and poor, but somehow or another I could still be one of Santa's dolls." I wasn't going to allow other peoples' opinions of me get in the way of my wants and needs.

My mother ended up buying me a dress that was yellow with white ruffles from the department store in town. She worked overtime just so she could do it.

I remember feeling so special the night of the Christmas program. My dress was the prettiest one of all; prettier than any that the snobby girls wore. Even one of the teachers told me so. My mother wasn't able to attend because of her work, but my sister and all my brothers did, and we told her all about it.

In many ways, I feel like my whole life has been similar to a Big Thicket—lots of thorny obstacles that are tough to get around. But the day that I stood up for myself and told the world what I really wanted to be gave me the courage to keep on doing it. All things considered, I've done pretty well.

I sometimes wonder what would have come of me if I had settled for being an elf or a reindeer.

Chapter 13

OF ROSES AND THORNS

A certain man planted a rose and watered it faithfully.
Before it blossomed, he examined it.
He saw a bud that would soon blossom.
He also saw the thorns, and he thought,
"How can any beautiful flower come from a plant,
    burdened with so many sharp thorns?"
Saddened by this thought, he neglected to water the rose,
    and before it was ready to bloom, it died.

So it is with many people.
Within every soul, there is a rose.
The "God-like" qualities planted in us at birth, growing
    amidst the thorns of our faults.
Many of us look at ourselves and see only the thorns.
We despair, thinking nothing good can possibly come
    from us.
We neglect to water the good within us,
    and eventually it dies.
We never realize our potential.

Some don't see the rose within themselves.
It takes someone else to show it to them.

One of the greatest gifts a person can possess is to be able

to reach past the thorns and find the rose within others.
This is the truest, most innocent, and gracious
    characteristic of love –
    to know another person, including their faults,
    to recognize the nobility in their soul,
    and yet still help another to realize they can overcome
        their faults.
If we show them the rose, they will conquer the thorns.
Then will they blossom, blooming forth thirty, sixty, a
    hundred-fold as it is given to them.

Our duty in this world is to help others, by showing them
    their roses and not their thorns.
It is then that we achieve the love we should feel for
    each other.
Only then can we bloom in our own garden.

- Author Unknown

SECTION FOUR

TOADS AT WORK

Chapter 14

NANCY'S DILEMMA

*Man's power of choice enables him to think
like an angel or a devil, a king or a slave.
Whatever he chooses, his mind will create and manifest.*
- Frederick Bailes

Nancy's story:

During my second year living in Las Vegas, one unusually cool August morning stands out in my mind. I was studying hotel management at UNLV, and, to apply what I was learning, I was working for a middle-grade hotel chain at a property just off the strip.

A husband and wife team managed the hotel, and they had their only son, Josh, working for them. His mom worked as the manager, his dad as the maintenance man. Josh's dad, Mr. Smythe as he insisted we call him, was a rough man who barked orders as if he was a crew chief on an oil rig. No tact. Sometimes even the customers received the brunt of his bark. I'm sure that he wasn't helping his business all that much, even though he thought he sounded important.

Josh's mom kept the hotel books, and she made sure every employee knew that she managed the place. But Josh was something special. At 23, he was still quite immature, and had acquired a keen ability to tune out his parent's words. His parents nagged at him constantly, but it was obvious that he became immune to it long ago.

On this particular day, I heard Josh walk in the side door by the office. "Another day in the salt mines," I heard him mumble. "Great," I thought. "Another workday with Mr. Wonderful. Well, I'll make the best of it." I was used to Josh being complacent and irresponsible. Working in a hotel was definitely not his cup of tea—he was there only because his parents owned the place. Besides, I was graduating next year so I wouldn't have to work with him forever.

I was at the front desk helping guests, working to make sure everyone felt special when Josh walked up and stood next to me. Guests were lined up six deep, but he just stood there watching me as if nobody else was in the lobby. I wanted to ask him to help, but his mom was beside me doing paperwork, and I didn't need to be scolded again for telling Josh what to do. "You're not his boss," his mom had told me on more than one occasion. So, I kept on helping guests as efficiently as I could.

90

After a few minutes, one of the guests walked into the lobby from our complimentary breakfast area and came up to the front desk. "You're out of coffee," he said. I smiled and replied, "We'll be right there."

I knew better than to ask or tell Josh to go check. I turned to Mrs. Smythe and said, "We're out of coffee, and I'm helping customers here. Who would you like to refill the coffee?" I had learned how to get things done.

She sighed without looking up. "Josh, go check the coffee," she said.

Josh copied her sigh, and I fought the desire to roll my eyes. What a Toad-filled family!

Josh walked around to the breakfast area, and I cringed when I heard him bark out, "You folks aren't supposed to be rummaging through the cupboards like that."

I thought to myself, "Not only is that no way to talk to guests, but they wouldn't be rummaging through the cupboards if you would take some initiative and do your job!"

Based on Josh's comment, I could just imagine the disaster in the breakfast area. I had been stuck behind the counter for almost an hour while Josh showed up late and his mom dealt with paperwork. Customers were sitting down to wait for coffee as Josh walked off with empty coffee pots. Ten minutes later he reappeared with coffee and then came back around and stood behind the front desk again. This time it was me who gave the heavy sigh.

Half an hour later, the front desk traffic died down enough for me to go check on the breakfast area. It was appalling—a total disaster. Plastic spoons were on the floor amidst spilled coffee and orange juice. The counter top was littered with sugar, coffee stirrers, empty creamer packets, and more spilled coffee and orange juice. The napkin holders were empty, as was the container for plastic ware. No cereal bowls were available. Glancing to the food items, I noted that the cold cereal was almost empty, as were the jelly packets and the cinnamon rolls. I looked for styrofoam cups and found none.

I got pretty miffed at Josh, who wasn't doing anything but standing around. "What is this guy's problem?" I wondered. I decided to let Josh and his mom handle the front desk.

In ten short minutes, I restocked and cleaned the breakfast area so it looked fresh and ready to go, just like it did at 5:00 a.m. "What is so hard about this?" I thought.

Just then Mr. Smythe came into the breakfast area. "This area closes in ten minutes!" he barked. "Get what you need and get out." The guests looked up in astonishment, and I cringed in embarrassment. "Only a few more months," I thought. "Then I'll be free from these Toads!"

Thoughts:

Is it possible that Josh is squirming through life with only minimal effort in everything he does? It appears that Josh is experiencing a stream of family Toads that are affecting him on the job. For example, Josh's parents don't hold him to any level of professionalism. In fact, Josh's parents seem to have quite the diversified Toad collection: Control Toads, Complacent Toads, Barking Toads, Ignoring Toads, and probably the ever unpopular Task-Only Toads, where people-skills are left out of the picture for the purpose of completing a task. And they certainly aren't encouraging Josh to find the occupation of his calling.

Nancy, on the other hand, has a good grasp of what Toads are and how they prevent forward motion. Hats off to Nancy. By the way, it is important to point out that people are not Toads: People have Toads. People can act with Toady behavior, but they themselves are not Toads.

Chapter 15

THE TOAD IN SHEEP'S CLOTHING

Our doubts are traitors,
And make us lose the good we oft might win
By fearing to attempt.
- William Shakespeare

Tony always dreamed of being a chef. With that in mind, restaurant work was all he ever did. He started out as a prep cook and worked occasionally as a head cook in eateries around the Baltimore area. By his early twenties, he'd saved enough money to attend a well-respected school for the gourmet training he wanted. After that, he only worked in upscale restaurants, eventually becoming a head chef. Over the years, he built up an extensive repertoire of tasty, original dishes. The tall and lanky Tony absorbed many tricks of the trade and became highly respected among his peers.

Now, just before his fiftieth birthday, Tony was fulfilling a lifelong ambition by opening his own restaurant. It was a nice place not far from a military base on the east coast. It would mean long hours, but this was his chance to realize his dream. Adding to Tony's excitement was the "partnership" aspect of having his daughter, Rana, on-board. She was the only family he had left after his wife was killed in a car crash a year and a half earlier.

Tall and slender, and an artist in her own right (a painter who had studied in Paris), Rana had beautiful blonde hair that framed her face like an award-winning portrait. Even so, Rana was shy and preferred the solitude of a studio. She talked with her father several times, telling him she'd rather not work at the restaurant, but Tony persisted. He convinced her to be one of the servers and help out as a hostess in the evenings. "It will save us a lot of money," he said. She preferred to spend time in her studio, but, despite her strong desire not to work in the restaurant, she never said another word about it. She was hesitant to rock the boat against her father's dream so soon after her mother's death.

Unbeknownst to Rana, a Sabotage Toad had jumped into her head, hiding its true identity. It fooled her into wearing a pleasant demeanor, whispering for her to play the role of supportive daughter. But deep down other things were happening. The Toad was playing with Rana's mind.

"Tony's Place" opened on a warm day in May. Overall, things went well. Tony spent a lot of time experimenting with new dishes, getting inventories established, and keeping the books.

But one thing Tony lacked was a head for marketing. All of his years in the business had been spent in the kitchen. It was there that Rana's Sabotage Toad saw its chance—it told her to forget about marketing. It whispered, "Just serve good food and be pleasant." As a result, Rana told her father that spending money on marketing was a risky idea. She didn't believe promotions would increase the restaurant's business; they would just cost them money.

She never vocalized her Toad's beliefs to the employees, but behind the scenes Rana exerted a lot of influence on how Tony thought.

You can guess what happened. After a year of marginal growth, Tony's business slipped into a slow, steady decline. Not knowing what to do, Tony spent more time in the kitchen and became skittish about spending any money on advertising. The Toad was doing its job well: Tony now believed every penny was necessary for survival. He thought, "What if we spend money on advertising that doesn't pay off? How will we pay our bills?"

One of the restaurant's regular customers was Steve, an experienced advertising and marketing consultant who entertained clients at Tony's Place several times a month. Tony found out what Steve did for a living and began to pick his brain as to why more people weren't coming into the restaurant.

"It's definitely not because the food is bad," commented Steve, "This is by far the best food in town." The two of them became friends and spent some time evaluating the situation. Steve liked Tony and wanted to see the restaurant succeed, so he took it upon himself to help Tony out in exchange for a few meals.

Tony had no advertising budget to speak of, so the first thing Steve did was design some discount coupons. "You need to print up a few thousand of these," Steve said.

Later that night, Tony showed the coupon to his daughter. "Oh my," she told him, "Every time someone uses one of those coupons we're going to lose money." Rana printed up only one hundred coupons. She convinced her father that too many coupons would be too costly. "Our profits will go way down if we start doing this," she said.

The next week when Steve came in for lunch with a client, Tony stopped by the table. "Those coupons didn't work," he said. Steve felt blindsided, especially in front of his client. After Tony walked away, Rana came over to the table to serve them. She was polite to Steve and thanked him for designing the coupons.

Over the next year, Steve offered Tony lots of solid marketing advice. Usually Tony loved the ideas, but he always came back to Steve a few days later with some restriction on the promotion. All along, Rana treated Steve with the utmost respect and courtesy, thanking him for his efforts in promoting the restaurant.

The Sabotage Toad won its largest coup when Steve suggested advertising in the military base's newspaper. Tony liked Steve's idea: A "two-for-one" Tuesday lunch special. Steve didn't wait. He placed the ad that day.

The morning the ad broke, Rana was concerned about how much money they were going to lose. She thought the officers had enough money to buy lunch at full price, so the discount should go to enlisted soldiers only. Tony went along with her logic, but didn't say anything to Steve.

That Tuesday the restaurant was full for lunch. Rana was one of the servers, and she asked to see the military ID of everyone requesting the special. Several tables of officers got up and left in disgust when Rana told them the special was for enlisted soldiers only. A few officers pointed out that the ad mentioned no such restriction. Rana politely apologized, but they made loud comments of not ever coming back.

When Steve heard about this his jaw hit the floor. "Don't you want more business?" Tony parroted the logic his daughter presented him, but Steve couldn't believe his ears. It was unfathomable to him.

After this fiasco, Steve decided he couldn't help Tony anymore. He was a professional who made good money because of the results that came from his advice. Yet here, despite practically giving his services away, Tony wasn't enjoying the success his other clients enjoyed. Steve felt he was fighting a losing war with all his strategies being changed by the time they got to the front lines.

Steve stopped going to Tony's Place. So did many others. The Sabotage Toad had done its job.

On an unusually cold night in September, Tony hung the "Closed" sign on the door for the last time. A month later, Tony and his daughter moved to New York where Tony took a job as executive chef at a three-star restaurant and Rana spent a lot of time catching up on her painting. The Sabotage Toad, having done its work, then went out looking for another victim.

Thoughts:

Again, remember that people are not Toads: They have Toads. And though people may harbor and nourish Toads, they're not always conscious of it.

In this story, Rana was unable to recognize her desire to set good boundaries and pursue her own calling. When the Sabotage Toad took up residence, it invited its favorite buddy, the Passive-Aggressive Toad, and the two worked together flawlessly to achieve their aims. Rana wasn't even aware they were around.

100

Tony had some Toads of his own. Although it's hard to say without closer examination, he might have been feeding a Co-Dependent Toad. While he might have been lonely after his wife's death, he should not have coerced his daughter (his last connection to his wife) into restaurant work, something God had not called her to do. Her grudging compliance was not good for either one of them.

Tony also had a Short-Sighted Toad, which prevented him from seeing the positive ripple effects of marketing his business.

When two people are feeding Toads within themselves that feed off each other, a swirling vortex is created that keeps the Toads in a symbiotic relationship, making them hard to eliminate.

Toad Funeral #5

Chapter 16

A MATTER OF FOCUS

Finish each day and be done with it.
You have done what you could.
Some blunders and absurdities no doubt crept in;
forget them as soon as you can.
- Ralph Waldo Emerson

Marshall's story:

The time was 2:29 in the morning. I had locked the liquor doors a half-hour ago, and the convenience store where I worked night shift was now quiet. On the outskirts of a major metropolitan area, the 24-hour convenience store was the place to get something if you wanted it after the supermarkets closed. Beer and wine were the big sellers in the wee hours of the morning, and after 2:00 a.m., when liquor sales had to stop according to state law, store traffic slowed to a crawl.

In between jobs and looking for a new direction, I had taken the night shift position so I could regroup from my recent divorce and decide where I wanted to go with my life. At 24 years old with no kids, I had been living the party life with my friends, but after my wife left me for my best friend, I decided it was time to grow up. The university was only two miles away, and I'd been thinking about going back to school to get a degree in either engineering or firefighting. My dad was a firefighter back east, and if I chose to follow in my father's footsteps, it might be a signal to my parents that I was finally "coming around." When I was a kid I loved to hang around the station house, so the thought of becoming a firefighter was rolling around in my head.

With no one in the store, I walked over to the magazine rack. I figured on taking a fifteen-minute break during which time I'd read an article or two from the latest edition of Popular Science, and then start in on the nightly clean up and restocking rituals. As I walked back behind the counter I nodded to a sandy-haired, blue eyed kid who walked into the store, and then I began flipping through my magazine as I leaned against the counter near the register.

A minute later the blonde young man walked up to the counter with a six pack of soda and set it down. Instinctively I straightened up and started pushing register keys without even looking at the customer. "Will that be all for you?" I asked. As I looked up, the young man was pointing a gun straight at me. "Open the register," he said.

"Oh gosh," I thought, "this kid can't be more than seventeen or eighteen years old!" I stared at the kid with disbelief. This couldn't be happening!

"Open the register!" yelled the kid. I didn't want to give him any money, but I didn't want to get shot, either. I figured if he was going to get any money, he'd have to take it himself. I pushed the key on the register that opened the drawer and stepped back with my hands up at shoulder height. "If you want the money," I said, "you take it."

The kid raised the revolver right up in my face so close I could see the bullets in their chambers. "Get on the floor!" yelled the kid. I turned, got down on my knees and started to get on the floor. Every second seemed an eternity as I thought about all that I'd done wrong in my life and how I'd wished I'd done things differently. I thought about my failed marriage, losing my previous job, all the fights with my parents, everything. I thought about fishing with my dad, and never being able to catch anything decent. My mind raced. I had a sinking feeling that the cold tile floor of a convenience store would be the last thing I'd ever see. I could hear the kid taking the money from the cash drawer, and since I had seen the robber's face, I figured it was mere moments before a bullet would enter my brain and either end my life or make me a permanent vegetable.

Then it got quiet, and I couldn't tell what the robber was doing. Was he stealing lottery tickets? Taking cigarettes? I felt tortured, waiting there to be killed.

Suddenly I heard a voice. "Are you okay?"

The voice belonged to an older man, not the robber, and I wasn't sure what to do. "Are you okay?" the man asked again.

I slowly moved my head around and looked up at the man. "What are you doing on the floor?" he asked. I stood up and told him I had just been robbed. "I'm going to have to ask you to leave the store," I said.

After calling the police and my manager, I tried to collect my wits. My manager came in and reviewed the security videotape with the police, and then told me I'd done a good job. I thought otherwise. I knew that store rules stated that I was supposed to cooperate totally with the robber, and treat the robbery just like any other transaction. But I had resisted, and in so doing, risked my life. I couldn't get the sight of that revolver out of my mind. I had done so many things wrong.

My manager stayed and helped me with the rest of the work, which I appreciated. He offered to let me have a few nights off, but I told him that the next night was my regular night off and I thought I'd be okay.

The next morning I crawled into bed at 8:30 a.m., which was my routine after getting off the night shift. Just as I was dozing off to sleep, I awoke with a start. Sitting straight up in bed and breathing fast, I was terrified. I dreamt a revolver was pointed in my face. "It's just a dream," I said out loud, "just a dream," and I lay back down. Ten minutes later, the same thing happened again. Over and over, throughout the morning and into the afternoon, I woke up every ten or fifteen minutes because of a gun in my face. Obviously, I didn't get much sleep. Thank God I had the next night off.

Tired of the recurring, heart-pounding dream, I got up, showered, and went for a walk. I couldn't stop thinking that I hadn't followed company procedures and it had almost cost me my life. I kept thinking that maybe if I had been more alert instead of reading that magazine I wouldn't have been held up.

Back in my apartment that night I watched TV, hoping to doze off. I was exhausted from no sleep and my body clock was off. Eventually, by midnight, I started dozing, but I kept waking up startled, dreaming about a gun being stuck in my face.

No matter what I did or what I tried to focus on, I kept dreaming about that stupid gun, and it kept me from sleeping for a second night.

The next day, after no sleep, I called my grandfather who lived a few miles away. I needed something. Even sleeping pills weren't helping.

I walked over to Grandpa's house, told him about the robbery, and that I couldn't sleep because of my recurring dream. "I just keep thinking about how much I screwed up," I told him.

"You gotta stop letting this eat at you from the inside," Grandpa said. "I hear you repeating over and over how you did things wrong. You got this little voice in your head telling you what you did wrong and it's blocking you from focusing on what you did right."

I didn't say anything, but I must have looked puzzled because Grandpa continued.

"If I'm not mistaken, don't those stores have a policy for what to do in case of a robbery?" I nodded. "Here's what I want you to do," he said. "Tonight, when you go back to work, I want you to locate that list of things to do and write down everything you did right. Don't focus on what you didn't do—focus on what you did right and make me a list."

I didn't have any better ideas, so I followed Grandpa's advice. At work that night I was on my toes. Every person who walked in the door was a potential robber, and I kept my eyes on everyone like a hawk. After things slowed down I did as Grandpa suggested. I made a list of things I'd done right during the robbery. To my surprise, the list was quite long. I had not totally resisted. I had let the robber take the money. I had closed the store after the robbery. I had called the police. I had called my manager. I didn't let anyone disturb the crime scene. I didn't touch anything that would destroy any fingerprints from the robber. Overall, my list of what I did right was a whole lot longer than what I had done wrong. I felt better almost immediately.

The next day I got off work at 7:00 a.m. and headed straight home to sleep. And sleep I did! I slept from 8 in the morning until 9 at night, never once waking up with any nightmares. Well-rested, I went back to work the next night at 11 p.m. and enjoyed myself the whole night through. The next morning I called Grandpa. I told him that his assignment had done the trick and that I had slept like a baby with no nightmares. "Keep it up," he told me. "Stay focused on what you're doing right."

And I do. Whenever that little voice of self-criticism tries to take over, I now know how to shut it up.

Toad Funeral #6

Chapter 17

WHY WRAP HAMBURGERS IN PAPER?

*All truths are easy to understand once they are discovered;
the point is to discover them.*
- Galileo Galilei

Bob's story:

As a sales rep, I travel more than I'd like to. My wife and kids are "on their own" several times a month while I'm away, but the job pays well so I stay with it. Recently, I managed to schedule two presentations in Pittsburgh on the same day—one in the morning and one in the afternoon. That way I could fly there early in the morning and get back in a one-day trip.

On the morning of the flight, I found myself wishing it were an overnighter. I needed a day or two away. My eight-year-old son had been a handful lately and I was a little exasperated with him.

111

It was a relief to leave the house that morning. I flew in to Pittsburgh early and had my first meeting done by 11:00 a.m. As I was packing things up, I realized I'd forgotten some papers back at the office, and therefore needed to stop at a copy shop before my afternoon appointment. I politely declined a lunch invitation and headed to the office supply store. By noon, I had what I needed and decided to stop by a fast-food restaurant, grab a quick lunch, and study up for my afternoon presentation.

Two minutes after sitting down to eat and review my notes, I heard a little girl's voice. "Why do we use these trays?" Although she was not yelling, her lungs were obviously strong and her voice carried well. I must have been sitting 30 feet from the register area and she was loud and clear. I looked up to get a glimpse of this vociferous little girl and then went back to my work.

Less than a minute later, I heard her again: "Why do they wrap the hamburgers in paper?" My thoughts drifted away from my work, and I couldn't help remembering fielding questions like that from my own kids. "Whew! I'm glad I don't have to do that anymore," I mused.

Then, the fact that I had to go back home that night and deal with my eight-year-old gave me an unsettled feeling. I pushed the thought away and felt a little sorry for the girl's father who was escorting her through the crowded

112

dining area. I felt a sharp twinge of aggravation when this little brunette with the powerful lungs and her father sat down at the table next to me. "Why do we use straws?" she asked, as she pushed her straw through the slot in the cup lid.

I fought giving a scowl to this little girl with the insistent questions, struggling inside to think through my afternoon presentation. Question after loud question popped out of this girl's mouth, one every five seconds: "Why do they put lettuce on hamburgers? Why do they put pickles on hamburgers? Why is bread brown? Why is ketchup red?" My focus was blown out of the water.

The questions went on and on, incessant, non-stop, and everlasting. Not only could I not focus on my notes, I couldn't even think my own thoughts. In a matter of minutes, I was fixated on what question this girl would ask next. The questions kept coming and coming.

Frustrated, I thought about getting up and moving to my car where I knew I could have some peace and quiet. As I sat contemplating how to regain my sanity, I suddenly heard something else besides the girl's questions: I heard her father's responses. It was like something switched in my brain. I sat up a little straighter and paid closer attention.

After each unrelenting question, the father responded in a quiet and respectful way, giving concise answers in a

113

loving tone. Never did his voice sound exasperated or condescending, only loving and accepting.

At this point, her sheer inquisitiveness and his loving, respectful responses pushed the Toad of Intolerance out of my head. My mind shifted from being distracted to being intrigued. This was a wonderful example of good parenting.

Whether or not the father knew it, his respectful responses were nurturing in this little girl a natural curiosity. I pictured her twenty years from now, confident that her questions were valuable and important, and that she would get deserved answers.

This little girl was not going to go through life feeling repressed or diminished. Her approach to life would be one of empowerment and inquisitiveness, a life where she feels like she's worth something and her initiative matters.

I closed my notes for my afternoon meeting and smiled. I made a mental note to pay more attention to my own son's questions, and to respond in a loving, respectful tone. That would start as soon as I got home, and I was suddenly glad I was going home that evening. I wrapped up the rest of my hamburger to go and left to find a phone so I could call home.

Note:

We often carry around Toads that raise their ugly heads when we think our "space" has been invaded. Although privacy is a good thing (and a healthy thing), we grow the most when we reach out and look at other's perspectives. It is too easy for us to get caught up in our own worries while neglecting the needs of those around us.

The little girl in this story was learning initiative—how to be confident and creative in exploring the world. Her father was doing a great job of creating a Toad-Free environment for her.

The sales rep was sensitive enough to see past his own Toads and, as a result, experience growth as a parent and a person.

Toad Funeral #7

Chapter 18

THE TOAD IN THE PIANO

What is dangerous about the tranquilizers is that whatever peace of mind they bring is a packaged peace of mind. Where you buy a pill and buy peace with it, you get conditioned to cheap solutions instead of deep ones.
- Max Lerner

Dressed to elegant perfection, Julie, a pianist, was providing accompaniment for a tenor at his master's degree recital. The audience was over two hundred music professors and graduate musician students at a major university in the northwest. The selection, by Brahms, was a dramatic story of star-crossed lovers who are separated but then united at the end. A challenging piece both technically and artistically, the pianist and tenor had so far given exemplary performances. The performance had gone without blemish until the last of the sixteen songs, when perfection was ruined at the last second: Julie hit a wrong note in the final chord.

Mortified, Julie immediately corrected the chord, but the mistake was obvious and glaring, especially in front of a musically-informed audience. She stared at the face of the now silent piano as the audience gave polite applause. She envisioned a saw coming up through the stage floor, sawing a circle around her that she would fall through to take her away from the site of her embarrassment. A wonderful performance was marred by this singular, glaring mistake.

Her next performance, a violin and piano recital, was only a week away. She dreaded it, but what could she do? She was under contract and she had to perform. Would she once again flub the final note and ruin someone else's recital? The Toad grew and grew in her mind until it took over her waking life. It sat there, waiting for her diversionary tactics to weaken for even a second, and then it would wrap her in its mind-numbing anxiety.

Julie, herself a master's degree student, took her fear of yet another public humiliation to one of her professors. He told her not to worry, and suggested that she take beta-blockers, a drug to relieve anxiety. He assured her that many musicians dealt with their performance fears by taking drugs. He confided that this is what he did to deal with his performance anxiety.

She considered that possibility briefly; it would make her life so much easier. But after thinking it through, she refused to avoid the Toad in that way. She felt that it was cheating—that performing artists need to learn how to face and deal with their Toads. She wanted to face her particular Toad with a clear, albeit frightened, mind.

Going into her next performance, Julie was extremely nervous. She kept envisioning that last chord where she would hit a wrong note. During the entire recital, she did fine, until that last note and her hand came down on the keys to make the final sound. She felt the hesitation in her downward stroke. Her fingers hit the keys a bit too slow. Although the chord was correct, she knew that she had failed artistically—that the Toad of Anxiety had checked the optimal flow of her performance.

The mistake was not really noticeable, except to her. But she had managed, through the force of her own will, to push her fearful mind and body past the weight, power, and will of the Toad. It had tried to trip her up on that final chord, but she had suppressed the desire of that little demon.

Julie's next performance was a little easier—and the one after that even easier. Eventually, the Toad died a natural death. All that remained were the normal performance jitters.

Note:

Looking back, Julie wondered what would have happened if her contract hadn't compelled her to perform again so soon after that single, glaring mistake. She had wanted to quit to avoid the power of that Toad. Powerful it was, for it had taken over her mind at its inception. If left to grow, it might have become a permanent crippling force, but she had faced it and conquered it soon after its emergence.

Julie, now a piano teacher, tells her students about that Toad and how she faced and killed it. It helps her students understand that she is not infallible, that such things are part of being a performance artist. Most importantly, being a professional means having the character and courage to deal with Toads without denial or drugs.

Chapter 19

THE TOAD IN THE LOBSTER*

A lobster,
When left high and dry among the rocks,
Has not instinct and energy enough
To work his way back to the sea,
But waits for the sea to come to him.

If it does not come,
He remains where he is and dies,
Although the slightest effort
Would enable him to reach the waves,
Which are perhaps within a yard of him.

The world is full of human lobsters:
Men stranded on the rocks
Of indecision and procrastination,
Who, instead of putting
Forth their own energies,
Are waiting for some grand billow of
Good fortune to set them afloat.

- Dr. Orison Swett Marden

*Note: This is our title for Marden's poem. Our search revealed no title for it, so we provided one that we liked.

SECTION FIVE

TOOLS FOR TOAD KILLERS

How can we recognize and kill the Toads that inhabit our heads? Reflection is one way to identify and understand our Toads, but we can't stop there. An obstacle identified does not make an obstacle removed.

The following chapters offer tools and techniques for not only identifying the Toads in your life, but for eliminating them as well.

As with any toolbox, you won't need to use all the tools all the time. A plumber uses a pipe wrench only when he needs it. Same with an allen wrench and a socket wrench. All are wrenches, but each is used for specific purposes at specific times.

The same is true of the tools in this section: All are useful, but you won't need every tool for every job.

Chapter 20

ESTABLISH TRUE FRIENDSHIPS

*Friendship is the process of refining the
truths each can tell one another.*
- Adrienne Rich

It is hard for us to see our own Toads. This is illustrated in a line from Joseph Heller's best-selling novel, *Catch 22*: "You can't see the flies in your eyes if you have flies in your eyes." Therefore, a key tool for Toad killers is to establish true friendships. Friends help us spot the Toads hiding and lurking around in our minds. But having true friendships also means being a friend. If someone is trying to hide from a Toad, say a drinking problem, and you collude with that denial, then you are an enabler, not a friend.

Too often we call people friends who really are only buddies or acquaintances. Good friends are those that can safely point out Toads to each other. They also help devise ways for turning them into carcasses. But friendship requires trust. Therefore, one of the best things to do to build good friendships is to be trustworthy. Then choose as friends other people who show themselves trustworthy. After all, we don't want to discuss our Toads with just anybody.

It can be easy to see Toads in someone else. Sometimes too easy. This is especially true if someone has upset us, if we're insecure, or if we have a reason for distrust. Sometimes, we can even see Toads that aren't there! For this reason we should be cautious: We are responsible for our perceptions. If we construct imaginary Toads in other people, that says more about us than them.

On the other hand, sometimes it is hard to see Toads in our friends. At least two reasons exist for this:

1. We don't want to risk the static of pointing them out.
2. It says something about us if we have Toad-filled friends.

But love—yes, love—says that we must be aware of the Toads in our friends and have the courage, concern, and consideration to point them out. Love means being patient and kind with ourselves and others. It means being polite, yet truthful. It means we don't get envious of our friends' blessings and good fortunes—or too proud of our own. Love says that we accept others and ourselves as people who have Toads, but we care so much that we don't want ourselves or others to be diminished by those Toads.

Pointing out a Toad to a friend requires creating an emotionally safe environment. After all, nobody truly enjoys hearing negative things about themselves. Therefore, remember that people are not Toads, people *have* Toads.

When you start talking about a Toad in someone else's life, you may want to start by bringing up how the Toad seems to be holding that person back. If your friend starts getting defensive, we suggest backing down to allow for a little venting. Here are some good things to do if that happens:

a)   Keep quiet and pay attention,

b)   Show love and concern in your facial expression, not disagreement or judgment,

c)   After the other person calms down, paraphrase what the person says without agreeing or disagreeing.

Showing this level of patience can be difficult, but it is part of what good friends do. If the friendship has any kind of mutual trust at all, the truth—and forward progress—will eventually win out.

If a friend approaches you about a Toad, remember that it's in your best interest to hear it out and give consideration to your friend's comments. Yes, it may hurt, but sometimes the truth does. As it says in the book of Proverbs, "faithful are the wounds of a friend; but the kisses of an enemy arc deceitful" (Pr. 27:2). A true friend has your best interests at heart. You may choose to ignore the friend's comments, but if someone else makes similar observations about you, well, you may actually have the Toad!

Finally, don't be too picky, for we all have Toads. (Where else do all of our warts come from?) Many Toads simply make us a little quirky. But we should learn how to help kill the ones that cripple and diminish the life and potential of our friends, and ask them to do the same for us. True friends help us see our Toads.

Chapter 21

USE STORIES

*Reconnecting people to their wisdom or common sense
is difficult to explain in objective terms...
...story can deliver, build, and sustain faith.*
- Annette Simmons

A good tool for Toad killers is stories. Read about the lives of people. Listen to their predicaments. Think about them. Reflect on their struggles. The recognized value and effect of stories is why we wrote the first part of this book the way we did: People can learn much from the experiences of others. The more stories we know about the different kinds of Toads people face and how they can be dealt with, the better able we are to recognize our own Toads and rid ourselves of them.

As a society, we are beginning to reconnect back to the power and worth of stories. Narrative learning in education and narrative therapy in psychology are growing movements. Ministers continue to use object lessons today just like Jesus used parables some 2000 years ago. Stories help us perceive the patterns of ourselves. They are an excellent way for humans to learn because they help us construct meaning.

Even secular stories often contain sacred meanings to help us ascertain our place in the scheme of things. They can help us identify and eradicate Toads, especially the systemic ones that like to hide from everyday awareness. Stories connect us to ourselves, others, and our spiritual health.

Chapter 22

GAIN EXPERIENCE

*Good judgment comes from experience;
experience comes from bad judgment.*
- Author Unknown

In the previous chapter we recommended that you learn from the experiences of others. But perhaps more important is the capacity to learn from your own predicaments. Gaining experience is not as simple as having something happen to you.

What does it mean to gain experience? Some background on the word *experience* will help us answer this question:

In ancient Persia, there were stories about malevolent spirits that lurked in the forests. Whenever people were so unlucky as to encounter one, they could get hurt, even crippled, or sometimes, even die. An evil spirit was known as a "peri." That word jumped over to the Greek language, and, from there, to Latin. The word "peri" now forms the root of such words as peril, perish, expert, and experience. Etymologically, the word "experience" means to escape a danger. It does not mean to possess a certain body of knowledge, as is a common misuse today. Experience indicates the accumulation of wisdom from having faced and, most importantly, worked through, perilous situations. Experienced people are ones who have dealt with their Toads in a courageous and healthy way. An expert is, regardless of paper credentials, someone who has gained experience.

One of the skills in Toad killing is developing your judgment about who has (and who has not) gained experience. Experience has to be gained. It has to be constructed. Some people can stumble into situations from now until Doomsday and not learn anything from them.

To identify someone with experience, listen to a person's language. Is it victim language, or does it speak of lessons learned? And if it speaks of true lessons learned, has the person built and maintained initiative, or is the language full of reasons to "avoid?" Your answers to these questions will let know you whether or not you're dealing with someone who has truly gained experience.

But again, it is important that we learn from our own predicaments. If we regularly avoid difficult situations we lose opportunities to learn from them, and we remain unequipped to kill certain Toads. This is not to say we should go out looking for or creating difficult circumstances. Rather, when such situations do arise, we gain experience only when we face the troubles and actually work through them.

Chapter 23

BE AWARE OF YOUR ENVIRONMENT

*You are a product of your environment. So choose the environment
that will best develop you toward your objective.*
- W. Clement Stone

R ecall the questions asked of Mr. Centipede by the
Toad: "How do you walk with all those legs in
perfect unison? How in the world do you manage to move
them all, much less at the same time?" These are reason-
able questions that could have been asked out of intellectual curiosity. Regardless, Mr. Centipede's mind put the
questions into a feedback loop that resulted in paralysis.

In actuality, we do not know whether or not the Toad
had evil or disruptive intent with his questioning. Some
Toads aim their weapons out in the open, others are good
at camouflaging their evil intent, and some things we at-
tribute to Toads may not be Toads at all.

The same is true in the people around us. While our adversaries may assail us with Toady rhetoric, our best friends and loving parents will occasionally ask us questions like, "What compelled you to do that?" These are not necessarily questions originating in a Toad's mind; they could be questions asked by genuine friends and concerned parents. Yet at the same time, our friends and parents may be the caretakers of Toads.

For this reason, we need to be aware of our environment and how we're making decisions—both our mental environment and our physical environment.

Mental Environment

Internally, we need to choose what we listen to and how we listen to it. The responsibility for our mental life is always our own. As my (Dan's) step-daughter is fond of saying, "Growing old is mandatory, growing up is optional." When the apostle Paul was teaching about personal responsibility, he said, "When I was young, I spoke as a child and acted as a child. Now that I have grown, I have put off childish things."

As adults, we must make choices about what we will do. For example, we choose whether to take things personally or objectively. We must also learn to check things against the resonance of our spirit.

Additionally, in a very real sense, our ability to listen accurately to ourselves is tied to our alignment with our vocations. Check your thoughts with your spirit. If they don't fit, it may be time to choose something different.

Physical Environment

Remember that even though people may behave in Toady ways, people are never Toads, people *have* Toads. Therefore, we should frequently be in touch with our intuition about people. Some pack a lot of Toads, some not so many. (Yes, and some are actually Toad free!)

Good deer hunters will tell you that when hunting, they don't necessarily look for deer—they look and listen for something different in the environment. Aside from the obvious indicators like tracks and droppings, they stay aware of other factors: Broken twigs appearing on low-hanging branches; the sound of a hoof hitting a fallen log; bushes that "rustle" in a direction opposite the wind.

The same principle applies to Toad hunting. When a Toad is close by, you may sense that something is out of balance in the environment. Become aware of the indicators. In so doing, you increase your awareness of potential obstacles.

The following is a non-exhaustive list of possible indicators:

Personal Indicators:

Non-specific anxiety	Habitual resentment
A habit of defensiveness	Frequent fear or anger
A sense of depression	Low energy levels
Loss of sense of humor	Habit of procrastination
Inefficiency	Inability to sleep
Inability to relax	Chronic back tension
Loss of sociability	Withdrawal from others
Lack of passion	Lack of enthusiasm
Feeling insignificant	Fear of solitude

Social Indicators:

A deep sense of distrust	Lethargy
A sense of victimhood	A "CYA" mentality
Reduced productivity	Tense conversations
Negative synergy	Excuses and scapegoating
Lack of cooperation	Lack of laughter
A stressed atmosphere	A bureaucratic culture
Not feeling part of the team	Lack of shared vision
Undue hesitation	Excessive wariness

If any of these indicators appear in your life, they may indicate the presence of Toads. If you identify any such signs, get ready for a Toad hunt!

Chapter 24

IDENTIFY YOUR VOCATION

People of genius do not excel in any profession because they work in it, they work in it because they excel in it.
- William Hazlitt

Doing something you are not designed to do is fertile ground for the emergence of Toads. This was illustrated in chapter 13, The Toad in Sheep's Clothing. A woman worked in a restaurant when she was meant to be an artist, and the ripple-effect may have cost her father his dream.

In his book *Let Your Life Speak: Listening for the Voice of Vocation*, Parker Palmer says "the pilgrimage toward true self will take time, many places, and years."

Pay attention to the fit between your essential self and your situations. If what you are doing doesn't get easier and easier, then it indicates that what you are doing does not fit God's design for you. We are supposed to continually grow, to increase our competence and connection to our chosen endeavor, to become ever more capable of facing new challenges. If these things are not true, then you may be doing the wrong thing.

As a former San Diego Teacher of the Year commented at a workshop some years ago:

The first ten years I went to school in the morning all enthusiastic, and then trudged home in the afternoon feeling like a drained battery. Now, it's the reverse, I go to school to get reinvigorated.

That meant that the teacher was doing what God meant for him to do, even if it took him a few years to figure it out! Also consider this story about a little known dancer:

Just before it was time for the dance she had rehearsed for months, something grabbed hold of her legs, saying, "Don't do this. Don't go out there and perform this dance. Do something else."

But she was supposed to dance! Still, the voice came forth within her again, louder and louder. The voice spoke confidently, sure of its connection to her essential self. And the voice was completely free of Toads.

For years she had trained herself as a dancer and had identified herself as an entertainer who danced. This night was the night her career was to begin: Amateur night at the Harlem Opera House. Her dance was on the schedule. Her routine was rehearsed. The music was in place. But there was a voice saying she shouldn't do it—she was not supposed to dance for all these people. The voice was actually telling her to sing. She felt it in her very essence. In the acorn of her soul and in the whole of her potential, she was a singer, not a dancer.

When the emcee announced to the audience that she was going to dance for them, she shyly but bravely caught his attention.

"Yes, young lady? Oh! Pardon me. Miss Ella Fitzgerald has decided not to dance for us. She will sing for us instead."

Four encores later, Ella Fitzgerald began her career as one of this nation's musical treasures.

The little-known dancer became a world-renowned singer. She could have easily mistaken that Toad Free voice as a Toad trying to stop her from success. Perhaps she had a relationship with God and could sense His guiding hand. Regardless, by listening to the voice of her vocation, she changed the world of music forever.

Chapter 25

DEVELOP INITIATIVE

Opportunity is missed by most people because it is dressed in overalls and looks like work.
- Thomas A. Edison

Toads do not thrive in environments filled with initiative (remember, they don't like movement). Initiative is toxic to Toads.

Therefore, one way to defeat Toads is to build up momentum by setting goals and working to accomplish them. You may need to start small, but a list of goals creates a caravan of initiatives that is focused and on the move. Initiative begets initiative.

With "The Big Mo" on your side, Toads will rarely show themselves, and, when they do, they are more easily identified and shoved aside. After all, momentum is a powerful force! You become a team unto yourself, and you will also attract people who wish to contribute to your enterprise, whatever it may be.

Psychologists often call this "flow" and its power is phenomenal. Just ask any basketball player who ever tried to put a Toad in the head of Michael Jordan.

Mentor Initiative in Others

No matter what your situation in life, be a mentor. Mentors excite and inform the initiative of others. But don't waste time and energy trying to mentor someone who is not ready to resonate with your message. That only produces static and disillusionment, which causes the birth of Toads in both mentors and learners.

A Cardinal Virtue

Initiative is a cardinal virtue. Without it we not only do less, we think less, we learn less, and we are less.

What Does Initiative Do?

Initiative goes beyond description. It takes risks. It has the ability, though not a compulsive need, to challenge the status quo. It can, at any time, leap out of the box. It strives to help others; there is an element of selflessness within those who possess it. Initiative not only starts, it completes. It operates from a principled base; strong values underlie its choices of action. It has the habit of "revi-

144

sioning" the ordinary; it looks at today's problems with tomorrow's eyes. Initiative excites and leads forth the energies of intelligence and commitment. It is therefore a cardinal virtue, for so much of what we value hinges upon its existence.

Initiative not only moves, it finds ways to flow. Its movement is not frenetic; initiative moves with purpose, whether it is emotional, intellectual, professional, personal, or spiritual.

Chapter 26

TAKE RESPONSIBILITY

To shun one's cross is to make it heavier.
- Henri Frederic Amiel

Don't accept self-defeating behavior in yourself. Don't wallow in self-pity. Accept boredom as a personal responsibility. Any mind that finds boredom in itself is one lacking imagination or curiosity. Watch out for narcissism; we like to center on our own issues and woes. Go out the door and help someone in some way. There is no greater gift to yourself.

As best-selling author Stephen Covey says in his book *The Seven Habits of Highly Effective People*:

Look at the word responsibility—"response-ability"—the ability to choose your response. Highly proactive people recognize their responsibility. They do not blame circumstances, conditions, or conditioning for

147

their behavior. Their behavior is a product of their conscious choice, based on values, rather than a product of their conditions, based on feeling.

Self-defeating behavior, like a Victim Toad, seeks to make you a victim, unable to respond in ways that bring you fulfillment.

One thing that endeared my wife to me (Dan) was her response when my stepson got involved in a playground fight in the fifth grade. The fight broke out between one of his friends and some other kids, but many kids close by got involved in the scrape. The school principal telephoned, informing my wife that her son was not to blame, but rather he was a victim in the situation. My wife cut him off, telling him that under no circumstances was her boy to be labeled a victim—there were actions he could have taken to avoid being involved in the fight. She was firm that he learn about taking responsibility.

The point is that no matter what the situation, we have the choice to engage or disengage. Disengaging from unhealthy situations—or choosing to engage in healthy ones—are ways of taking responsibility.

Chapter 27

SET GOALS

If you don't know where you are going,
you might wind up someplace else.
- Yogi Berra

E arlier, in the chapter on developing initiative, we mentioned the need to set goals. Goals and missions go together, but they are often confused, so we thought a chapter on goal setting would be appropriate. The main concepts as well as the details of goal setting are taught in myriad workshops by consultants and trainers worldwide. Other books specialize on the topic, so for this book, our purpose is simply to give you an overview.

Before goals are set, it is important to identify one's mission. A mission is a direction for one's life (personally) or a direction for an organization (professionally). Simply stated, a mission statement identifies the general direction desired.

Goals, on the other hand, are one-time achievable activities that lead us in the direction of our mission. The two work together like this:

Mission: The direction in which we're going.

Goals: Clearly defined, realistic, measurable actions that support the mission and have a deadline.

When writing goals, we advocate using the S.M.A.R.T. acronym:

S—Specific. Clear and easy to understand.
M—Measurable. How long? How far? How many?
A—Action-Oriented. A verb that dictates our action.
R—Realistic. Is it sensible, rational, and practical?
T—Time-of-Completion. Goals must have deadlines.

The most neglected component of goal setting is assigning a Time-of-Completion. Consequently, many excellent ideas are never realized simply because no deadlines were created.

Even when deadlines are created, too often it's rush-rush-rush in the final minutes and hours. Perhaps you've heard the phrase, "if it wasn't for the last minute, nothing would get done." That's because Procrastination Toads slow us down. For that reason, we advocate creating mini-goals—milestones or checkpoints—to balance out our workload. This helps eliminate Procrastination Toads, which thrive when no deadlines are set.

Laura Crawshaw, founder of the Executive Insight Development Group and a Leadership Development associate, is fond of asking "by when?" She asks this so often that we associate her with that question! Laura understands the fundamental importance of including a time-of-completion when setting a goal.

Let us also emphasize that goals must be realistic. Undemanding goals fail to challenge us. Completing them is unfulfilling and leads to an apathetic mindset. On the other hand, goals set too hard lead to discouragement and grudging compliance.

Here are a few quick examples of good and not-so-good goal statements:

Not-so-good example: I want to make more money.

The statement is not specifically measurable (how much is more?), lacks a clear, specific action ("making" money is illegal – perhaps "earn" or "save" is better?), contains no time of completion (no "by when?), and we don't know if it's realistic because we don't know how much. Essentially, "I want to make more money" is a mission, not a goal.

Good example: I will save $4,000 before August 1, 20XX.

$4,000 is measurable. *Save* is our specific action. *Before August 1, 20XX* (you name the realistic year) is a specific time of completion. It meets the S.M.A.R.T. standards.

Another reason we emphasize setting goals is because doing so focuses us on where we want to go, and we always move in the direction of our focus. For example, in my younger years, when I would be riding my bicycle up a hill with a long incline, I (Dan) would often watch the pavement ahead of my front tire as I concentrated my energy on getting up the hill. Occasionally a rock would be in the path of my tire. I'd think to myself, "I'm not going to hit that rock ... I'm not going to hit that rock." But invariably, I'd hit the rock. Why? Because I was looking at the rock and my tire went where my eyes were focused. However, if after seeing a rock in my path I shifted my focus a few inches away from the rock, my bicycle tire went where I was focused, and I missed the rock.

This same truth is why driver's ed instructors tell us to "aim high" in the road. It keeps us aware of potential problems ahead (which we could equate to Toads), and keeps our car from moving erratically within our lane.

Bottom line, setting goals gives us a clear focus and a road map to follow. When we have such a map and we're focused on our goals, Toads are less likely to take us off course.

Note:

If one of your missions in life is to be Toad Free, then a good idea might be to write some goals for yourself based on what you're reading in this "Tools for Toad Killers" section.

Also, visit www.LeadershipAnswers.com for more information on goal setting.

Chapter 28

DO SOMETHING DIFFERENT

When you're finished changing, you're finished.
- Benjamin Franklin

We know too many people who complain of the doldrums, finding nothing to do but what they've always done, or they feel stuck, beating their heads against the walls of their circumstances. They feel trapped in their situations. They're stuck in the status quo and they don't like it. Toads, however, do.

In his book *Do One Thing Different*, Bill O'Hanlon advises us to develop a solution-oriented approach. He comments:

Whenever you are stuck with a problem, try something new. Do something—just one thing—different. Break the pattern of the problem. Insanity is doing the same thing over and over and expecting different results!

Mechanics know that having the right tool makes all the difference when trying to get something done. Hence, they're not afraid to get a different tool if what they're using at the time is not effective. In the same way, if what you're doing is not getting you past a bothersome Toad, consider trying something else. Some folks call this thinking outside the box.

If you're having a tough time thinking of alternatives, ask a friend. But be careful! Don't rationalize away why your friend's input won't work. Give it serious consideration and try it!   Doing something different may seem awkward, and may not even work. However, if nothing else, a different approach stretches our minds and opens our eyes to new ways around the Toads holding us back.

Bill O'Hanlon tells a story that illustrates the power of doing one thing different:

A favorite aunt of one of Milton Erickson's (a psychologist) colleagues was living in Milwaukee and had become quite seriously depressed. When Erickson gave a lecture there, the colleague asked him to visit the aunt and see if he could help her. The woman had inherited a fortune and lived in the family mansion. But she lived all alone, never having married, and by now had lost most of her close relatives. She was in her sixties and had medical problems that put her in a wheelchair and severely curtailed her social activities. She had begun to hint to her nephew that she was thinking of suicide.

O'Hanlon tells how Erickson visited the colleague's aunt and found her depressed and isolated. She had previously been an avid church-goer, but since being confined to a wheelchair, now only went on Sunday. The woman had only one joy in her life; a greenhouse nursery attached to the house. The aunt had a green thumb and her best hours were spent growing flowers. She was particularly fond of African violets.

The woman admitted to Erickson that her depression had become quite serious. His unique approach was to suggest she do one thing different.

O'Hanlon continues:

Erickson told her that he thought depression was not really the problem. It was clear to him that she was not being a very good Christian. She was taken aback by this and began to bristle, until he explained, "Here you are with all this money, time on your hands, and a green thumb. And it's all going to waste. What I recommend is that you get a copy of your church membership list and then look in the latest church bulletin. You'll find announcements of births, illnesses, graduations, engagements, and marriages in there—all the happy and sad events in the lives of people in the congregation. Make a number of African violet cuttings and get them well established. Then repot them in gift pots and have your handyman drive you to the homes of people who are affected by these happy or sad events. Bring them a plant and your congratulations or condolences and comfort, whichever is appropriate to the situation."

Hearing this, the woman agreed that perhaps she had fallen down in her Christian duty and agreed to do more.

Twenty years later as I [Bill O'Hanlon] was sitting in Erickson's office, he pulled out one of his scrapbooks and showed me an article from the *Milwaukee Journal*. It was a feature article with a large headline that read "African Violet Queen of Milwaukee Dies, Mourned by Thousands." The article detailed the life of this incredibly caring woman who had become famous for her trademark flowers and her charitable work with people in the community for the ten years preceding her death.

O'Hanlon informs us that either "changing the view-ing" or "changing the doing" of a problem in even one way can change a situation dramatically. We hasten to add that it can also kill Toads. Erickson's insight helped the woman kill the Toads of Depression and Isolation that were growing within her.

Bottom line, choosing to do something differently than the way you've been doing it can sometimes be enough to get past a Toad blocking your way.

Chapter 29

RELIEVE STRESS

Do not worry about tomorrow, for tomorrow will worry about itself.
Each day has enough trouble of its own.
- Matthew 6:34

S tress is a part of every person's life: Students are regularly under stress, stress is often found in the home, and stress often fills the workplace. Left unchecked, stress causes a ripple effect of problems, and it is, by nature, a breeding ground for Toads.

Take an inventory on how you relieve stress. Some common methods of relieving stress, such as watching excessive television, over-eating, or escaping through drugs or alcohol, end up producing bumper crops of Toads which—guess what—cause more stress! You end up digging yourself deeper into the mud.

According to Ellen Carni, writing in the legal journal *Forum*, one healthy approach to reducing stress is to write down all your routine tasks and your personal attitudes toward them. This does not have to be an ongoing activity, just do it over the course of a day or two. The simple exercise of writing out your thoughts helps you identify your mental framework. Like in the story A Matter of Focus (chapter 16), writing can focus you on what you're doing right—and help free you from Criticism Toads!

You can also journal about past situations in which you were successful at overcoming major obstacles. By mentally reviewing each situation as you make journal entries about them, you reinforce your achievement mindset, which gives you added integrity and reinforces winning strategies for upcoming pressure situations.

Another tip for reducing stress is to do your most difficult and uncomfortable tasks early in the day when you are fresh. Brian Tracy, in his book *Eat that Frog* (a different concept than Toad killing), outlines a healthy approach to prioritizing the difficult but important things that need to get done.

I first saw the analogy Tracy uses in his book on a T-shirt that I (Dan) bought for my dad many years ago. The artwork on the T-shirt was a guy stuffing a frog into his mouth, followed by the words, "If you eat a live frog first thing in the morning, nothing worse can happen to you the rest of the day." Tracy does an excellent job of drawing a parallel to getting unpleasant tasks out of the way first thing in the morning, and offers some excellent tips for doing so.

Procrastinating actually adds stress because the task you're putting off begins to fill your mind (much like a Toad does), and overcrowds your mental circuits as time goes on. Eat those frogs first thing in the morning and some of your Stress Toads will die a natural death.

Other stress-relieving activities include talks with good friends and time spent in recreation. Health care practitioners recommend ceasing all use of stimulants such as coffee or alcohol. (If you're a coffee-a-holic, shifting to ½ decaf and ½ regular may be an effective compromise.) Others recommend getting your office, your closets, or your pantry organized. Getting a pet is also a good idea. Research shows that pet owners have lower stress levels and actually live longer!

The following story highlights the importance of relieving stress as well as doing one thing different, the concept from the previous chapter.

One day I (Dennis) entered my classroom and began addressing the subject for the day. Soon, however, I noticed that one of my students, whom we shall call Carolyn, a young married mother of two, was upset. To my question asking if she was okay, she replied that she was consumed with anxiety because she was taking the state teacher licensing exam the next day.

Carolyn had studied and knew the material, but she was not a good test taker. She had taken the exam before and flunked. After she said that taking tests made her stupid (her word), I validated her point that test anxiety can block memory and stifle intelligence. The classroom conversation then shifted to people sharing examples of test stupidity.

The class was on human development, so the subjects of test anxiety and stress release were appropriate. The situation provided a teachable moment and I ran with it. I changed my agenda for the day to address test anxiety. We focused on how people choose to reduce stress in their lives. Examples ran the entire spectrum (the athlete exercises, the alcoholic drinks, etc.). We also talked about how the methods we choose to relieve stress define us in powerful ways.

I then asked Carolyn how she dealt with stress in her life. (I also begged her to not be too personal, which made her laugh.) She paused, and then gave a curious response:

"I don't have a way to relieve stress."

I responded with the following:

"Then, Carolyn, you will soon be a dead woman. Or, actually, you would already be dead (more laughter from Carolyn). Think about it. What is your primary method of relieving stress?"

"I guess I pray a lot."

"There you go. That works. Have you prayed about the teacher's exam?"

"Yes I have, but I am still anxious. I prayed before but I still flunked."

"What about a prayer circle? Have you asked for help from people in your church?" (I knew she was active in her church.)

"I can't do that," she said softly.

"Of course you can. They'd be happy to do it for you. Call some people together this evening. I've got ten dollars that says it will help you pass the test."

"I can't do that," she repeated.

At this point, one of her friends in the class joined the discussion: "But Ronnie (Carolyn's husband) can. I'm going to call him and ask him to pull together a prayer circle for you."

And she did.

Carolyn reported in the next class that after the prayer group had met, she had taken the test with a full night's sleep behind her and hadn't felt nearly as anxious as before. A few weeks later she caught up with me in the hall to inform me that she had indeed passed the test.

Not only did that particular day of instruction help Carolyn pass the teacher's exam, but the rest of the class saw the importance of relieving stress. It also contained lessons in the dynamics of test anxiety and the development of persistence; that is, not allowing oneself to become trapped by predicaments.

No matter what the stress, one can find a way out of it.

Chapter 30

SET HEALTHY BOUNDARIES

Givers have to set limits because takers rarely do.
- Irma Kurtz

B oundaries are put in place so we know who is responsible for what. We find them in suburban neighborhoods in the form of fences, in schools in the form of grade divisions, and at work in the form of offices and cubicles. Boundaries that are purposeful and solid keep lines of responsibility clear; boundaries that are falling apart do not.

In relationships, boundaries are the rules and cutoff points we put in place to protect ourselves. Think about the yellow lines in the middle of a road. These "boundaries" are for everyone's protection to keep drivers aware of where they should and should not be. Similarly, relationship boundaries can protect us from being "stepped-on," or prevent us from bowling over others with an overbearing attitude.

Christopher Avery, writing in *Training and Development* magazine, says that one of the keys to effective teams is to set and maintain healthy boundaries. The following scenario is offered by Avery:

> A team leader walks into a meeting eight minutes late. Everyone else was there on time. When the leader asked if everyone was ready to start, Ned, one of the team members, said, "No." Ned then confronted the team leader. "We all agreed to start and end team meetings on time. Everyone else was ready to start this meeting on the hour. Do we need a different agreement with you about this?"

How often do we get upset because other people fail to hold up their end of an agreement (e.g., always late for appointments, forgetting to do routine tasks, etc.)? Getting upset but not doing or saying anything about it creates Toad fodder. In the illustration above, it turned out that Ned's confrontation was accepted by the team leader as a valid action to maintain healthy boundaries within the team. The leader realized he was taking time from the team members—time the team did not want to give.

Every upsetting situation is an opportunity to learn. When people get mad, it's usually because they are mad at themselves. If you find yourself getting angry, check yourself. What is it that you did or didn't do? Usually you can find something to adjust within yourself. In other words, setting a new boundary. If you find you are upset at someone else's behavior toward you, it may be that you simply have not set a clear boundary. The solution? Set boundaries!

The courage to draw boundaries is a valuable skill that makes any home or workplace more effective. The book *Boundaries* by Dr. Henry Cloud and Dr. John Sims Townsend offers many helpful tips for establishing healthy boundaries in relationships. You'll find it listed in Appendix B, Good Reading for Toad Killers. If you have trouble setting boundaries, we highly recommend it.

Note:
   People who are unwilling to say 'no' and are always accommodating others' needs are often harassed by Guilt Toads and probably a few more. In addition to *Boundaries* by Cloud and Townsend, *When I Say No, I Feel Guilty* by Manuel J. Smith offers additional tips for setting healthy boundaries.

Chapter 31

BE INTELLIGENT

By wisdom a house is built,
and through understanding it is established;
through knowledge its rooms are filled
with rare and beautiful treasures.
- Proverbs 24:3

What does it mean to be intelligent? Forget standard IQ tests; they only measure memorization/retention, the capacity for language/math puzzles, and the ability to take tests. People with high IQ's have done a lot of stupid things.

One of the highest IQ's on record is that of a woman by the name of Tina Christopherson. She was bright to the tune of a 189 IQ. Nonetheless, she nourished one of her Toads into a monster, and it made her stupid. Here's what happened:

Tina was terrified that she would die of stomach cancer like her mother. To ward off this fate, she went on long fasts during which she ate nothing and drank great quantities of water. Sometimes she drank as much as four gallons a day. On February 17, 1977, she finally pushed her kidneys into failure at her home in Florida. Water migrated into her lungs, and she drowned on dry land at the age of 29.

The poor woman, even with an exceptional IQ, allowed a Toad to grow inside her mind to the point that it destroyed her.

While IQ measures one form of intelligence, Harvard psychologist Howard Gardner takes a different view. He says:

> Intelligence is the capacity to solve [real world] problems and fashion products.

According Gardner's perspective, Tina Christopherson lacked true intelligence. Despite her phenomenal IQ, she was unable to muster her brainpower to solve her problems or fashion the products that her brilliant mind was capable of constructing.

As we have seen throughout this book, Toads prevent the accomplishing of goals, the solving of problems, and the fashioning of products. Toads can make people stupid, no matter how much brain power God provided them.

How do we define stupidity? At the risk of oversimplification, we sum it up with an old Chinese proverb:

> When a finger points at the moon,
> the imbecile looks at the finger.

In other words, stupidity is the failure to perceive the significant. Much of the time, it is not lack of brain power but the presence of Toads that prevents us from realizing what is relevant in ourselves or our situations.

J. Martin Klotsche, former Chancellor of the University of Wisconsin at Milwaukee, said that:

> Intelligence is derived from two words—inter and legere—inter meaning "between" and legere meaning "to choose." An intelligent person, therefore, is one who has learned "to choose between."

Both Gardner's and Klotsche's perspectives are right. In striving to live Toad Free, we must look for Toads that prevent us from solving problems and choosing—usually Fear Toads or Lack-of-Information-so-Therefore-We-Can't-Decide Toads. Other Toads that get in the way of our intelligence are Delusion Toads, Lack-of-Courage

Toads, Complacency Toads, and the ever pernicious Go-Along-to-Get-Along Toads.

As Toad killers, we increase our intelligence by making wise choices. Yes, we will make mistakes along the way (see the next chapter about making mistakes), but if we are intelligent, we learn as we go. Even if we learn slowly, we're still increasing our ability to solve problems and fashion products, and eliminating many nasty Toads along the way.

Chapter 32

GO AHEAD AND MAKE MISTAKES

The man who makes no mistakes does not usually make anything.
                                    - Theodore Roosevelt

Everyone makes mistakes. New mistakes are opportunities for learning. Old mistakes (making the same mistakes over and over) form cesspools, which are breeding grounds for Toads. The key is to only make new mistakes. Once you make a mistake (and you will make them the rest of your life), learn from it and establish a new standard or boundary to prevent the mistake from happening again. Nothing prevents Toads from hanging around like eliminating their breeding grounds.

You will be well on your way to living Toad Free by following the advice of a wise old grandmother:

MAKE NEW MISTAKES—NOT OLD ONES

SECTION SIX

CONCLUDING THOUGHTS & STORIES

Toad Funeral #8

Chapter 33

You Polka?

To know oneself, one must assert oneself.
 - Albert Camus

A Personal Toad Story from Co-Author Dennis Rader:

I was born in East Tennessee into a nonacademic family. I never considered going to college until I was in my twenties. None of that bothered me in my teenage years. What troubled me was my pathological shyness.

I had a big Toad of Low Self-Esteem that squelched the volcanic pressure of my bubbling hormones. I simply could not talk to girls. That made it impossible to develop relationships, to ask them out, or even ask them to dance. I did, once or twice, go to school dances, but I would just hug the wall and eye the life on the floor. Dancing was a particularly large Toad in my life for some reason. It sure looked like fun, but my Low Self-Esteem Toad was so

Living Toad Free   Final Thoughts & Stories

powerful that I wouldn't even dance with myself—no bouncing in front of the bathroom mirror for me.

At age nineteen I left Tennessee and found myself in Cleveland working at a factory. I still blushed, mumbled, and occasionally stuttered in the presence of women that I found attractive.

A co-worker invited me to his wedding, but I didn't want to go. After all, people would probably be there! But he prevailed, and I went.

The reception turned out to be a surprise. In my Southern Baptist heritage, weddings were boring affairs. But this was a party. There was even an open bar, a new concept to me. And I have to admit, I consumed a few beers.

I was sitting with a few of my buddies from the factory when, suddenly, the mood of the place changed. The lights went down, tables and chairs were moved to clear a space, and a live band started making this kind of loud noise that I had never heard before. Immediately after all this, a giantess of an old woman was suddenly in front of me, asking a question:

"You polka?"

"What?"

"You polka?"

I didn't know what the woman meant. I did know that whatever it was, I didn't do it. So I said "No."

But this woman had no Toads in her. She loudly pronounced, "You polka!" and then pulled me out of my chair and dragged me out onto the dance floor.

Resistance was useless. The woman was my height but about 150 pounds heavier. Besides, she was ancient, at least to me, and she had this beautiful spirit about her. Hence, I was unable to get mad at her. She took control and whirled me around the floor to the raucous tune of the weird music. On a couple of whirls, I felt my feet leave the floor. I hung on to her because I didn't have any choice if I didn't want to go flying through the air. She smiled at me several times but primarily focused on her dancing.

My buddies left our table and came up to the edge of the dance floor. Whenever I was whirled by they hooted and hollered hysterically. They enjoyed my predicament immensely.

Then I got into it. What the hell! Why not? I began to dance. I even managed to smile at my buddies as I whirled by. I knew they would later rake me over the coals about my new girlfriend, but this polka stuff had an energy that just pulled me along. The first song finally came to an end (those polkas go on and on) and I thought the woman would let me go. But no way. She dragged me over to her family's table, then pulled this very beautiful but hesitant young woman (probably her granddaughter) to her feet.

The old woman forced my arm around the gorgeous young woman's waist. Dumb me, I actually resisted. Still insistent, she escorted us to the dance floor, and shoved us into the beginning music of the second dance. This time I had to lead, and to my surprise, I did. And did I love it! I also took great pleasure in the dramatically changed expression of my buddies when I circled by them the next time. Instead of gleeful derision, they responded with celebratory admiration.

Because of that evening, I became a dancing fool. Every night I found a place to dance. And I had to learn how to ask women to be my partners. I began to emerge from my pathological shyness.

I thank that woman, whoever she was. The life and joy in her infected me in ways she could never know. Her initiative carried me (almost literally) to a better life. The Toadlessness in her helped me learn how to kill some of my own.

Toad Funeral #9

Chapter 34

BLIND, BUT NOW I SEE

---

*That which is striking and beautiful is not always good;
but that which is good is always beautiful.*
- Ninon De L'Enclos

A Personal Toad Story from Co-Author Dan Bobinski:

I admit it: I'm a red-blooded, American male. My ideas of attractiveness were shaped in large part by Madison Avenue marketing. I paid entirely too much attention to outer beauty.

As a sad example, at one time in my life I met Jeanette, a slim, attractive, well-educated woman. We "clicked" quite well, conversing on many levels with ease. There was lots of chemistry, and we both knew we were interested in each other. But, since I was in a committed relationship at the time, I wrote off this beautiful lady as "the right woman at the wrong time."

A few years later, after a slow but amiable breakup with girlfriend number one, I contacted Jeanette for a date. She was available!

When date time came and I knocked on her door, a woman answered who looked nothing like the woman I remembered. I asked, "is Jeanette here?" "I'm Jeanette," she said, somewhat surprised.

I didn't say it out loud, but I thought, "Oh my God, what happened?" The woman with the chunky face before me looked 100 pounds heavier than the woman I remembered.

On our date that evening I could tell her interest in me hadn't wavered one iota since the last time I'd seen her. But I, on the other hand, bumbled my way through dinner, and later offered some lame excuse about being "just friends." Essentially, I weaseled out of anything more simply because of her looks. She told me that she was on a steroid medication that caused her to gain weight. Looking back, I'm ashamed at how superficial I was. Despite the strong intellectual attraction, I couldn't see myself being with her. At the end of the evening, I could tell she felt hurt.

I felt tremendously shallow and torn. But unknown to me, I was under the spell of a Skin-Deep Beauty Toad. I assumed beautiful on the outside meant beautiful on the inside, and I was only interested in looks.

184

As fate would have it, about a year later I ran into Jeanette again, and she looked even better than when we had first met. The extra weight was gone (she was off her medication) and she was a total knockout. In my stupidity, I tried to get a date with her, but to no avail. She would have nothing to do with me. (I deserved it!)

The Skin-Deep Beauty Toad continued to have a devastating effect on my life. I continued to be blind to inner beauty, only focusing on outward appearances. The woman I eventually married was slim and appealing. Unfortunately, I was blinded by her physical attractiveness and didn't see that her style and my style didn't blend very well. It didn't take me long to realize that I had made a huge mistake.

Not believing in divorce, I gave the marriage all I had. But struggling through that emotional tornado of a marriage was almost more than I could bear. Suicide passed through my mind more than I care to think. Eventually, after five marriage counselors and too many years of unbearable emotional turmoil for both of us, we split and finally divorced.

My divorce was an emotional roller coaster equivalent to a hurricane on steroids. But it was at this low point in my life that I finally saw the Toad. What was I to do? A person has eyes. There was no way to go through life and not notice beautiful women.

That was when I got a little radical: I prayed to God that I would become blind. I wanted to fall in love with a woman because of who she was, not because of her good looks. I needed to stop believing the lies of the Skin-Deep Beauty Toad! If I were blind, I reasoned, I would be able to hear her voice, absorb her words, and discover what she was really like on the inside. It was a three-quarter-serious prayer: I didn't really want to lose my sight, but I knew the Skin-Deep Beauty Toad was having a devastating effect. Still, I prayed.

God answers prayer in wondrous ways. In the early days of Internet chat rooms I was online chatting with some younger kids (in their late teens and early 20's) about marriage. Several chat room participants were recently engaged and excited about their upcoming weddings. After my divorce, I wanted to pass on a few tips, such as "don't buffalo your way through the premarital counseling," and "it is essential to take a very objective look at the way the two of you face problems."

During the conversation, another "experienced" voice joined in. This person spoke with intelligence, wit, and wisdom about relationships, but the person's chat handle was such that I didn't know if I was reading the words of a male or female. So, after a while, I asked. The response came back: "Female."

We chatted a while longer, and I learned that this woman had also come out of a difficult marriage. She was finishing college near the Rocky Mountains and had custody of her two kids.

We swapped email addresses and kept in touch. Coming home and checking for an email from her became something to look forward to. After months of emails and online chats, I became quite intrigued. I had no idea what this woman looked like, but I liked her sense of humor, her intelligence, and her balanced approach to life. I didn't care if she was 800 pounds with a beard, she was a wonderful person whom I wanted to know better.

Eventually we decided to meet. The place? Las Vegas. Half-way between San Diego and where she lived. The rules? Separate rooms. No commitments. No attachments. No hanky panky. Just friends.

Still not knowing what she looked like, I sent her an email offering her a huge safety net: I would meet her at the airport gate holding a single red rose. If she felt uncomfortable or unsafe in any way, she could just walk past me and I would never know who she was. If she felt comfortable, she could come up to the man holding the rose and introduce herself.

When her plane arrived, I stood by the gate, rose in hand. Scores of people streamed past me, and I began to wonder if she had walked past, or if she had even boarded her flight.

As I considered my options, a striking brunette walked up and said, "Hi." I couldn't believe my eyes. She was beautiful!

I introduced myself: "The name is Bond. James Bond." We both had a good laugh and then sat in an airport restaurant to talk for a while.

That weekend was like magic. It felt like we had known each other our entire lives. We stuck to our rules and thoroughly enjoyed each other's company. At the end of three days it was difficult for both of us to say goodbye.

As you might surmise, this story has a wonderful ending. More accurately, it is still being written. After continuing our emails, chats, telephone conversations, and seeing each other monthly, we realized we were in love. About a year later we were married.

Looking back, it is plain that God answered my prayer: I had met and had fallen in love with a woman without even seeing her. Essentially, I had been blind. Yes, my wife is quite physically attractive, but I saw and fell in love with her inner beauty long before I saw her outer beauty.

With that lesson, my Skin-Deep Beauty Toad was starved out of existence.

Chapter 35

THE ROOM OF 1,000 TOADS*

*Most of our obstacles would melt away if,
instead of cowering before them, we should make
up our minds to walk boldly through them.*
- Orison Swett Marden

Sammy Centipede was nervous. By special invitation he was attending a gathering of centipedes that hoped to gain enlightenment. He was standing rank and file with all the other centipedes, dressed in their ceremonial white socks and white tennis shoes. The lead centipedes lined up before the students, and then the high priest centipede flowed out of his cave. The whole scene, already silent, became focused as all eyes and ears turned to the high priest.

"This is the ceremony of the Room of 1,000 Toads," the high priest announced. "It is a ceremony to achieve enlightenment, and it occurs only once every 100 years. If you choose not to go through it now, you will have to

189

wait another 100 years. To help you make this decision, we will tell you what the ceremony involves.

"In order to enter the Room of 1,000 Toads, you simply open the door and walk in. The Room of 1,000 Toads is not very big. Once you enter, the door will close behind you. There is no doorknob on the inside of the door. To get out, you will have to walk all the way through the room, find the door on the other side, open the door— which is unlocked—and come out. Then you will be enlightened.

"The room is called the Room of 1,000 Toads because there are one thousand Toads inside. You should know that these Toads have the ability to take on the form of your worst fears. As soon as you enter the room, the Toads will take on the appearance of everything that frightens you and holds you back. If you have a fear of heights, a Toad will get under you and appear as a narrow ledge of a tall building. If you have a fear of spiders, the Toads will transform themselves into terrifying eight-legged creatures. Whatever your fears, the Toads will take on the appearance of those images in your mind and make them seem real. In fact, they'll be so compellingly real that it will be very difficult to remember that they're not.

"No one can come in and rescue you. This is part of the rules of the ceremony. If you choose to enter the Room of 1,000 Toads, you must leave it on your own.

190

"You should know that some centipedes never come out. They go into the Room of 1,000 Toads and become paralyzed with fright. They stay stuck in their fears until they die.

"If you do not want to take the risk of entering the Room of 1,000 Toads, that is fine. You do not have to enter the room. You can wait and come back in another one hundred years and try again. But my advice to you is: 'If you're not ready, get ready.'

"If you want to enter the room, we have two suggestions that will help you. The first is this: When you enter the Room of 1,000 Toads, remember that what they show you is not real. It's all just imagery taken from your own mind. Do not buy into it. It is an illusion. But keep in mind that every centipede that went in the room before you knew that. This is a very difficult thing to remember.

"The second suggestion has been more helpful for those centipedes who have made it out the exit door: Once you enter the room, no matter what you see, no matter what you think, no matter what you hear, *keep your feet moving*. If you keep your feet moving, you will eventually get to the other side, find the door, and come out. Then you will be enlightened."

Thoughts:

The bottom line to this analogy is *keep your feet moving*—keep doing something. We reiterate that everyone has motivation, but some people experience resistance and then stop moving. As we learned from Coach Hatfield, it is no sin to be blocked, only to stay blocked. Those centipedes that succeeded in their encounter with the 1,000 Toads are those that managed to have the wisdom, imagination, and willpower to hang on to their faith and their initiative. They never let their Toads freeze them into diminishment. By keeping your feet (and your intellect) moving, you cannot be stopped!

*The Room of 1,000 Toads is an adaptation of The Room of 1,000 Demons, from Do One Thing Different by Bill O'Hanlon. It has been rewritten to fit the Toad concept in Living Toad Free with permission.

Chapter 36

FINAL THOUGHTS

I set before you life or death, blessing or curse.
Therefore, choose life.
- Deuteronomy 30:19

The Toad concept is built around the insight of a simple poem (see chapter 3). It should be noted that the concept works regardless of one's religion, philosophy, gender, political party, or worldview. It works for both dog and cat people, and it doesn't matter if you drive a foreign or a domestic car, or whether you prefer paper or plastic.

Although we acknowledge that human beings should do everything in their power to get past their Toads, some Toads exist that can only be removed with a little spiritual assistance. If you ever have difficulty squashing, starving, or getting around a Toad, it can be a good idea to ask "Upstairs" for help! Happy Hunting!

APPENDIX A

WHERE THESE STORIES COME FROM

The stories in this book—Toads at Home, Toads at School, and Toads at Work—are all true. Most have been collected from students and clients over the years as we've shared the Toad concept and encouraged people to write about overcoming obstacles. We should point out that all names, places, and otherwise identifying points within a story have been changed to protect the innocent – and the guilty.

All sources have given us their expressed permission to use these stories in *Living Toad Free*. We gratefully acknowledge their willingness to expose their Toads and share how they struggled. It is our hope that each reader will learn from these stories and use them to help eliminate Toads from their own lives.

If you would like to submit a Toad story of your own for consideration in a future *Living Toad Free* book, please send it to us using either Email or snail mail. Your story should illustrate how you faced and overcame a

Toad in your life, or helped someone else overcome a bothersome Toad.

Submit your stories via Email to:

stories@livingtoadfree.com

Or submit them via snail mail to:

Leadership Development Press
ATTN: Toad Stories
P.O. Box 4082
Boise, ID 83711

If you have questions, call us on the toll-free Toad Free hotline: 877-TOADFREE.

Want to read more about Toads?
Want to receive the monthly Toad Free E-Letter Update?
Visit www.LivingToadFree.com

APPENDIX B

GOOD READING FOR TOAD KILLERS

Hundreds of resources are out there to help you in your quest to live Toad Free. The following list is by no means exhaustive; however, reading these books will help you in your pursuit to be a proficient Toad killer:

Boundaries: When To Say Yes, When To Say No, To Take Control Of Your Life by Henry Cloud and John Sims Townshend (Zondervan, Grand Rapids, MI, 2002).

Do What You Are: Discover The Perfect Career For You Through The Secrets of Personality Type by Paul D. Tieger and Barbara Barron-Tieger (Little, Brown and Company, Boston, 1995)

Please Understand Me II: Temperament, Character, Intelligence by David Keirsey (Prometheus Nemesis Book Company, Del Mar, CA, 1998)

When I Say No, I Feel Guilty by Manuel J. Smith (Bantam, New York, 1985)

The Seven Habits of Highly Effective People: Powerful Lessons in Personal Change by Stephen R. Covey (Simon & Shuster, New York, 1990)

The Seven Habits of Highly Effective Teens by Sean Covey (Simon & Shuster, New York, 1998)

Success! The Glenn Bland Method: How to Set Goals and Make Plans That Really Work by Glenn Bland (Tyndale House Publishers, Carol Stream, IL, 1972)

Eat That Frog!: 21 Great Ways to Stop Procrastinating and Get More Done in Less Time by Brian Tracy (Berrett-Koehler Publishers, San Francisco, 2002)

Do One Thing Different and Other Uncommonly Sensible Solutions to Life's Persistent Problems by Bill O'Hanlon (William Morrow and Company, New York, 1999)

Flow: The Psychology of Optimal Experience by Mihaly Csikszentmihalyi (Harper & Row, New York, 1990).

Understanding How Others Misunderstand You: A Unique and Proven Plan for Strengthening Personal Relationships by Ken Vogues and Ron Braund (Moody, Chicago, 1995).

The Death of Common Sense: How Law is Suffocating America by Philip K. Howard (Random House, New York, 1994).

Something More: Excavating Your Authentic Self by Sarah Ban Breathnach (Warner Books, New York, NY 1998)

The Bondage Breaker by Neil T. Anderson (Harvest House, Eugene, Oregon, 2nd Edition, 2000)

Overcoming the Dark Side of Leadership: The Paradox of Personal Dysfunction by Gary L. McIntosh & Samuel D. Rima, Sr. (Baker Books, Grand Rapids, Michigan, 2003)

The Bible (choose your favorite version!)

TOAD FREE PRODUCTS

Order your TOAD FREE merchandise today!
Visit www.LivingToadFree.com
or call toll free: 877-TOADFREE

NO TOADS lapel pin $ 5.95
The colorful "Toad Free" logo!

Living Toad Free Coffee Mug $ 7.95
White, with the color 'Toad Free' logo

'Certified Toad Killer' Parchment Certificate $ 4.95
(personalized with your name on it!)
    with Wood Frame $ 11.95

Desk Display $ 15.95
*Silver metal angled "nameplate" style holder
with Coach Hatfield's favorite saying (It's no sin
to be blocked – Only to Stay Blocked) engraved
on your choice of background colors.
10" across by 2" high.*

8x10 Engraved Coach Hatfield Plaque $ 39.95
*Choose between oak or walnut stain with
Coach Hatfield's favorite saying engraved
on brass (choose black or gold brass):
"It's no sin to be blocked - Only to stay blocked"*

See more Toad Free merchandise on our website!
www.LivingToadFree.com
Note: Prices subject to change

HOW TO SCHEDULE A TOAD FREE WORKSHOP

Tired of excuses?

Want to see more initiative?

Are you ready for a Toad Free workplace?

Bring a *Living Toad Free* Workshop to your place of business! Your employees will learn to identify and eliminate obstacles to motivation—propelling your organization into a more natural energetic flow. Increase your productivity! *Live Toad Free!*

(You can also schedule a Toad Free school assembly or a Toad Free seminar for your church!)

Call us on the toll-free Toad Free hotline:
877-TOADFREE
Or send us an Email: workshops@livingtoadfree.com

We'll help you knock your Toads out!

ABOUT THE AUTHORS

Dan Bobinski, M.Ed.
Email address: dan@LivingToadFree.com

Dan Bobinski is a certified behavioral analyst who holds a Master's Degree in Education (with a Human Resource Training and Development emphasis) from Idaho State University and a Bachelor's Degree in Workforce Education and Development from Southern Illinois University, where he graduated summa cum laude.

In addition to conducting workshops nationwide on management, leadership, communications, and customer service, Dan writes an internationally-published weekly column on workplace issues, titled *Answers for the Workplace*. Dan is a past-president of the American Society for Training and Development Eastern Idaho Chapter, and he appears in *'Who's Who' in American Executives and Professionals*.

Dan developed a love for teaching while serving in the U.S. Navy in the early and mid-1980's. He has been president of Leadership Development, Inc. since 1989. He currently resides in Boise, Idaho.

Dennis Rader, Ed.D.
Email address: dennis@LivingToadFree.com

Dennis Rader holds a Doctorate in Education from the University of Massachusetts in Amherst, and a Bachelor's degree in Psychology from Oberlin College in Ohio. Dennis wrote the first doctoral dissertation in the United States on the subject of personal integrity.

Dennis is an author, storyteller, and college professor who lives in a cabin way off in the woods of Southeast Kentucky. He has a series of books coming out with Rodopi Press on postmodern philosophy in education. He is currently finishing up his novel, *Bugscuffle*, and his book, *Hogs on Ice: Thoughts About Student Motivation*, which helps teachers understand student resistance to the educational process.

Dennis walks to the pond by his cabin most every day, keeping a wary eye out for any toads that may be lurking in his path, accompanied by his dogs, Jasper and Jubilee, and sometimes even by his cat, Gracie.

Printed in the United States
101273LV00005B/1-18/A

9 781594 674808